The Illustrated Book of Runes

©Dawn Steeves 2020

FIRST EDITION — 2021

All rights reserved. No part of this publication may be reproduced, distributed, or transmitted in any form or by any means, including photocopying, recording, or other electronic or mechanical methods, without the prior written permission of the publisher, except in the case of brief quotations embodied in critical reviews and certain other noncommercial uses permitted by copyright law.

Stock purchased from Adobe
'Breath Fire' typeface commercially licensed through Chequered Ink Ltd. by Thoughtweft Publishing Inc.

BOOK COVER, DESIGN AND LAYOUT: Stephen Ikesaka
COPY EDITORS: Freya Aswynn, Stephen Ikesaka, and Reikhart Odinsthrall
ILLUSTRATIONS: Dawn Ravenwind
PUBLISHED BY: Thoughtweft Publishing Inc.
                   Kelowna, British Columbia
                   http://aetherphoxx.wixsite.com/thoughtweft

ISBNs: Hardcover 978-1-989013-11-3, Paperback 978-1-989013-12-0

The Illustrated Book of Runes

Dawn Ravenwind

Thoughtweft Publishing, British Columbia

Table of Contents

2. What are the Runes?
10. Biography
13. The Art and Myth
18. Other Notes

126. Using the Runes
127. Choosing the Runes
130. Daily Practice and Relationship Building
133. Crafting Talismans & Writing in Runes

142. Rune Casting
148. Conclusion
151. Bibliography

The Aetts

22. Freya's Aett
    24. Fehu
    28. Uruz
    32. Thurisaz
    36. Ansuz
    40. Raidho
    44. Kenaz
    48. Gebo
    52. Wunjo

56. Heimdall's Aett
    58. Hagalaz
    64. Nauthiz
    68. Isa
    72. Jera
    76. Eihwaz
    80. Perthro
    84. Algiz
    88. Sowilo

92. Tyr's Aett
    94. Tiwaz
    98. Berkano
    102. Ehwaz
    106. Mannaz
    110. Laguz
    114. Ingwaz
    118. Dagaz
    122. Othala

Acknowledgements

This book could not have been created without the help of the larger community. I was inspired to create it from the encouragement of The Asatru Community and Runes for Runesters Facebook groups. The Illustrated Book of Runes was then funded through the Kickstarter community and the 138 backers that supported my project by pre-ordering books and prints. Thank you all so much for your generosity and trusting in me and my book.

Thank you to Freya Aswynn, Reikhart Odinsthrall and Stephen Ikesaka for reviewing and editing my manuscript.

From my personal life I would like to thank Dustin for building my beautiful companion website (www.ravenwindillustration.com) and being there throughout the crazy year I spent illustrating and writing this book. Thank you also to little Ragnar, for being a constant source of inspiration and wonder who continually challenges me to grow as a person. And lastly, to all of my friends (Kristen, Heru, Robyn) who have helped me with various parts of the project, particularly filming and editing the Kickstarter video.

I wish to express my gratitude to the Aesir and Vanir, whose stories and archetypes provide continual lessons, wisdom and inspiration; especially to Odin, for the discovery and knowledge of the Futhark runes.

The narrative for the Runes is modeled on The Hero's Journey of Joseph Campbell. This put a nice Jungian underlay of the Runes. This book will be very helpful for those of us who do counselling as well as divination. Personally, there is no difference.

—FREYA ASWYNN, AUTHOR OF NORTHERN MYSTERIES AND MAGICK

What are the Runes?

I believe most of you have an idea of what runes are. The word "rune" brings to mind primitive inscriptions, rough lines sketched into wood and stone. They can be seen as a historical alphabet, but for those of us who are embracing modern paganism the runes are far more than that. They are a system of magick, a field of philosophy, a way of understanding psychology and a link to embrace and understand our pagan ancestry.

At its foremost, a rune is a letter. It is a visual symbol that represents a particular sound, exactly like an alphabet. The German verb "raunen" translates as "to whisper." A whisper is a soft sound, but it also implies secrets and mystery, as we often whisper messages when we don't want them to be heard by everyone.

Runes were used by many ancient European peoples but are made famous today by their use in Norse cultures. The Elder Futhark (Futhark being the first six runes in the alphabet) is the primary runic alphabet that is used now and originated in the area now known as Germany. The tribes there developed a written script based upon a Roman one, perhaps even Latin, as they had been recruited into the Roman military and afterwards brought home the idea of written language. The Elder Futhark eventually branched into multiple other runes, including the Younger Futhark, the Anglo-Frisian Futhorc and the Armanen runes.

The Germanic tribes no longer survive to this day; they were indigenous peoples whose culture was lost when Christianity conquered Europe during the Crusades. The people themselves, including their language and physical features, developed with the land they inhabited. Their myths, like all indigenous cultures, were entwined with the forces of nature that the people were subject to, such as the changing of the seasons. From these myths came respective deities and many stories to explain the natural phenomenon.

The runes are intimately linked to the forces of nature, and you can gain perspective into the lives of the Germanic tribes by learning the runes and understanding their mythos. Early peoples were subject to natural forces in a way that was much more in tune with our planet than we are today. Hail could be devastating, a forest fire even more so. The animals they raised and relied on for survival, such as cows, goats and horses, had a sacred value. Creatures of the forest, benevolent or otherwise, such as wolves and ravens, were also incorporated into myth, as these creatures were rarely seen but often treated as omens or portents when they appeared. The runes can help guide the western materialistic culture back to some of our lost indigenous roots by reuniting us with these natural forces.

According to old myths, the runes were discovered by the god Odin. The story goes that Odin had sacrificed himself upon his own spear and hung himself upside down from the tree of life, Yggdrasil, for nine days and nine nights without food or drink. At the end of this trial, it is said he saw the runes in the fallen branches that lay upon the ground and was given one of the highest forms of wisdom when he took them up.

The following are verses 138-145 in the Havamal, the sayings of Odin, as found in the *Poetic Edda* translated by Carolyne Larrington:

I know that I hung on a windy tree
nine long nights,
wounded with a spear, dedicated to Odin,
myself to myself,
on that tree which no man knows
from where its roots run.

No bread did they give me nor drink from a horn,
downwards I peered;
I took up the runes, screaming I took them,
then I fell back from there.

Nine mighty spells I learnt from the famous son
of Bolthor, Bestla's father,
and I got a drink of the precious mead,
poured from Odrerir.

Then I began to quicken and be wise,
and to grow and to prosper;
one word found another word for me,
one deed found another deed for me.

The runes you must find and the meaningful letter,
a very great letter,
a very powerful letter,
which the mighty sage stained
and the powerful gods made
and the runemaster of the gods carved out.

Odin for the Æsir, and Dain for the Elves,
Dvalin for the dwarfs,
Asvid for the giants,
I myself carved some.

Odin is a figure of great myth, postulated as possibly being based upon a real shaman that had once lived and, perhaps, did invent the runes. Ancient stories of Odin and the other Norse gods and goddesses were passed down in oral tradition as poems and stories and had never been written down until Medieval times.

These stories undoubtedly changed slightly with each retelling, significantly with each generation, and vastly over millennia. It is a work of imagination to guess what these tales were originally based upon, but it is generally accepted that the ancients created tales as ways of understanding the universe, nature and our own psyches. It was a way of passing wisdom between generations that united and entertained both young and old. Whether Odin was a real human or born of this need to understand natural forces, the tales about him and his kin are a timeless wisdom that people from all walks of life can take meaning from.

The runes, whether you see them as provided by Odin or entirely born of Roman lettering, enabled a written language that opened many possibilities for the ancient Germanic peoples. Written language is not only a powerful tool, but it was also seen as having magickal properties. Words carved upon a surface could be translated and understood by people in the future. Germanic peoples at this time did not have paper and ink, so were limited to inscriptions in wood, metal and stone. It was a seemingly magickal way of communicating by sending messages through space and time to other people.

King Harald rune stone, 10th century Jelling Denmark

But perhaps more importantly, the ancient Germanic peoples found magick in each individual sound and letter combination. Each sound was represented by one rune, one symbol. The sounds of the language were important vibrations that could be chanted and sung by their shamans. When sung this way, the chants are called *galdr,* and were seen as powerful tools for magick and connection to their gods. The symbols were also meaningful. These symbols were tangible representations for each magickal property the sound had, and the message and vibration could then be conveyed through visual means.

For example, the F rune (ᚠ)is called Fehu and vibrates as an 'f' sound. The shape of Fehu is said to be two cow horns, and the symbol of Fehu is the cow. Cattle were an important aspect of wealth, and the simplest way to transcribe the magickal meaning of Fehu is wealth itself.

Every word, every song and every piece of writing these ancient peoples created was thought to have magickal value. Words had value, especially written ones, but inscriptions were not as common as with many other European languages because they were used more for magick than just information. The amount of space and time required for carving runes also limited the length of the message.

The runes were also used on smaller scales as individual runes, rather than words and long messages. These are frequently found as talismans, such as amulets for protection. Many inscriptions can be found on swords and armour for blessings. Runes were also believed to be tattooed on people's bodies, despite a lack of archaeological evidence. There is indication in their history that they were, at the very least, drawn on people with magickal intent. Additionally, runes can be combined to make bindrunes, which have the magickal properties of multiple runes.

Divination might be the most popular modern usage of the runes, but there are few historical reports of such. I believe it highly likely that their ancient shamans, such as the *völva* of the Germanic peoples, would have used the runes for divination purposes despite the lack of records. Chance and fate were highly linked in their belief system, and a set of runes etched into wood, bone or stone had magickal properties that could help the shaman ascertain one's fate. We do have one frequently quoted passage from 98 C.E. where the Roman Tacitus, in his writing, *Germania*, gives an account of the Germanic people that suggests the use of marks (believed to be runes) helped guide choices and actions:

> *"They attach the highest importance to the taking of auspices and casting lots. Their usual procedure with the lot is simple. They cut off a branch from a nut-bearing tree and slice it into strips these they mark with different signs and throw them at random onto a white cloth. Then the state's priest, if it is an official consultation, or the father of the family, in a private one, offers prayer to the gods and looking up towards heaven picks up three strips, one at a time, and, according to which sign they have previously been marked with, makes his interpretation. If the lots forbid an undertaking, there is no deliberation that day about the matter in question. If they allow it, further confirmation is required by taking auspices."*

From ancient Germany, the runes moved north and became an iconic part of Nordic cultures that also took with them the tales of the Aesir. The Elder Futhark runes are known to have been used between the second and eighth centuries. The Scandinavian countries of Denmark, Sweden, Norway and Iceland all used forms of the runes, such as the Icelandic or Younger Futhark and the Anglo-Saxon (or Anglo Frisian) that had originated with the Germanic peoples. Standing runestones can still be found in their culture's homelands, as well as places they'd travelled, like England and Greece.

With the expansion of militant Christianity and the Crusades, which included persecution against the pagan Baltic, Finnic and West Slavic peoples, much of the history of the gods and runes were lost. Some people converted to Christianity, but many died in battles defending the old ways and their knowledge and wisdom died with them. What we have left is frequently the research of Christian scholars with a very different perspective than the people that lived and breathed a life that involved Odin and the runes. And while we have useful information recorded in works like the *Poetic and Prose Eddas,* we will never know what those authors refused to include and how much was changed because they disagreed with, or didn't relate to the ideas.

Snorri Sturluson was the first person to take the Norse stories that had been passed down by oral traditions and amalgamate them into a written form when he put together the *Prose Edda* (also known as the Younger Edda). This was written in Icelandic in the thirteenth century, long after Christian influences had diluted the culture and stories. However, it is the primary source of information on the old Norse tales that is used by scholars.

The *Poetic Edda* (or Elder Edda) is a combination of the poems that Snorri used to make his Edda. They were said to have been compiled by Sæmund the Wise somewhere in the tenth century. Brynjolfur Sveinsson, a Christian bishop, created the *Codex Regius* in 1643 from a manuscript that had a collection of twenty-nine verse poems that are believed to be from Sæmund. These included poems that were identical to those that had been used by Snorri. Any current renditions of the *Poetic Edda* are versions of *Snorri's Edda* and the *Codex Regius,* which are, again, a recent product influenced by a Christian point of view.

Despite the differences in religious perspective and the resulting bias, the *Poetic and Prose Eddas* are the best, most historical source that we have today to learn the stories of Norse mythology. They provide us with good insights into old Norse culture and the thought patterns of these earlier peoples.

The rune poems are some of the oldest existing resources for the runes. There are three of them: the Icelandic and the Norwegian rune poems, both using the sixteen-rune Younger Futhark system, and the Anglo-Saxon rune poem of twenty-six runes. The Anglo-Saxon rune poem dates back to the tenth century and is an invaluable resource that anyone learning the runes should study. It is the closest of the three to the Elder Futhark, as well as the oldest of the poems, though it was only revived in 1705 and thus has also likely lost some of its wisdom.

One small way the rune wisdom may have survived is through the tarot. There are many parallels between the explanations of the major arcana cards of the tarot and the runes, such as the symbolism of The Sun and Sowilo (ᛋ), The Hanged Man representing Odin hanging from Yggdrasil, The Wheel of Fortune and Jera (ᛃ), etc. This newer system of the tarot became very widely used.

By the middle of the fifteenth century, runes were no longer used as a writing system except for some isolated areas in Sweden and Iceland. The last recorded use of the runes as a community-based writing system was in the isolated community of Älvdalen, Sweden, which was still using runes just over a one hundred years ago. When sending children to school became mandatory this use was lost. They began using the "Dalecarlian" runes, based on a Latinized version of the Younger Futhark Runes. Some people in the region still speak Elfdalian, which is thought to be the most similar to old Norse of all existing descendant languages.

Part of the revival began in 1865 when Sophus Bugge in Norway had been studying previously collected runic artefacts and learned how to read the twenty-four-letter code. The name Futhark was created from the first six letters of the Futhark alphabet (ᚠ ᚢ ᚦ ᚨ ᚱ ᚲ) and has been used since to name this runic system. His studies focused solely on the linguistic aspect of the runes—what each symbol's sound was, and how to read inscriptions.

Though discovery of rune linguistics in the 1800s was a matter of academic curiosity, books on the Elder Futhark and its magickal properties only came long in the 1980s. Modern use of runes as a magick system came with Stephen Flowers, aka Edred Thorsson, and Freya Aswynn, both of whom came from different backgrounds and philosophies. The runic system that was recreated from these pioneers has inspired many books, and rune magick is almost a fundamental practice for the tens of thousands of Asatru (modern Norse paganism) followers in the United States alone.

There were a few other attempts at rune revival. Guido von List had written about the occult use of Armanen runes in the early 1900s. His system became linked to the Nazi-era belief of Aryan supremacy and was highly linked to the secrets of Freemasonry. For obvious reasons is not widely or openly used. Ralph Blum also wrote a book that is frequently purchased, most often by people who have never yet studied runes. Blum's book is widely discredited as he created his own order to the runes, consulted the *I Ching* for meanings that are often described as "fluffy," and added a "blank" rune that is often confusing to people learning but is still used by some practitioners today.

An important thing to remember is that the foremost property of the rune is the vibration. It is a frequency. Modern physics has discovered many powerful properties of frequencies, and anyone that enjoys or creates music can understand the potency of particular sounds. Modern psychology has also learned some of the mysteries of sound and energy, such as the kiki/bouba experiment, where participants were asked to name two very distinctive shapes: one of which had soft, rounded curves and the other sharp, pointed corners, as either "bouba" or "kiki." Regardless of their native language, 95% of the participants called the rounded shape "bouba" and the sharp cornered shape "kiki."

Both ancient shamans and modern practitioners of the runes are faced with the challenge of taking these vibrations and trying to use words, symbols and stories to explain these energies. It is not an easy feat; it is like trying to describe the colour red. This is why each account of the runes is different. It is why there is no one, singular description or meaning to each rune. And this is also why the best way to learn the runes is to use them, over and over, daily, and with many methods. Whatever else you do, don't just read one book or one account, as any singular explanation and perspective is biased in some way.

Hopefully, this brief summation of the runes has given you some insight on their ever-changing nature. Like any language they are dynamic, changing with each generation that uses them. It is important to learn the history of the runes and understand the roots from where they came. Modern use by occultists is the most recent change enacted upon the runes, but this gives them no less power than any previous generation as long as we honour them and take time to connect with the nature and ancient deities that birthed them. Knowledge and awareness of the runes continues to grow with each book that is written, and with each author that takes the time to learn the runes themselves.

Biography

I will now take the time to introduce myself. This is so you better understand my perspective, and why I created this book and artwork. The runes are a source of great inspiration for me and have become a daily guide to which I pay attention, similar to how ancient astronomers watched the stars. I have no doubts about the powers of the runes and their synchronous nature with the intrinsic and extrinsic universes.

I come from mixed Canadian ancestry, with Métis (French and aboriginal peoples mixed), German, Welsh, Scandinavian and probably several other sources mixed in. My ancestry has links to nature, shamanism and Germanic runes, making it a part of my history. But I don't think blood is nearly as important as my experiences themselves, which is where the real learning occurs.

I spent the first twelve years of my life on an off-grid homestead in the northern part of British Columbia. When I was born my parents lived in a tepee, a kind of Native American dwelling with sticks and a covering similar to a yurt, with a pointed roof and a fire in the center. Winter temperatures could be as low as -40°C, and snow sometimes stayed as late as June and came as early as September. I spent much of my time outdoors, wandering the forests with our wolfdogs, learning about survival skills and plant medicines. I developed a very strong bond with nature. We would eat eggs and vegetables we raised and grew, and have deer and moose meat when it was available. We would also supplement with other foods by going to town, about forty-five minutes away. Life was not easy, and it made me something of a hard person, but it gave me a unique perspective of the world, and what ancient European cultures endured.

As a teenager, I spent a great deal of time studying different forms of ancient paganism. I was drawn into the occult, and it became a home for my strangeness. I used tarot from the age of twelve and was gifted my first set of runes at eighteen. I practiced a type of meditation I had learned at the age of seven, which I later found out was a form of shamanic journeying, through which I commune with spirit animals, such as my dragon power animal. I spent time learning about energy fields, chakras, yoga, dream analysis, astral projection and anything I came across that sounded interestingly metaphysical. I later studied Zen Buddhism when I first went to university, which allowed me to step back from the intensity of what I had practiced during my teenage years and learned more of eastern philosophies and practices.

I did quite well in school. In high school my grades were top of many of my classes, and I excelled in most things. My mind has a balance of left and right-brained thought, so though I am an artist I am also inherently very good at logic and mathematical learning. I didn't enjoy the teachers, however, due to my independent nature. I decided to do distance learning for much of high school so that I could teach myself the information.

For university I decided to study Biology in Victoria, BC. I also took two years of German language studies during this time. I continued to do well academically, earning a Bachelor of Science with Honour's for my thesis on stickleback evolution, and Distinction for having grades within the top ten percent of graduates. I followed this up by working on a master's thesis in which I studied forest changes over 14, 000 years by analyzing fossil pollen in a lake core. I left school with an undefended MSc thesis already written and edited because of a combination of unsolvable issues with my supervisor, and to take time to focus on my pregnancy (and eventual family).

I moved to the Kootenays with my son, Ragnar, in 2015. Since my life seemed to be drawn away from science, I have mostly focused my energy on becoming an artist. I created a business called DragonheART, in which I create handmade chainmail costume pieces, many of which have scales incorporated, called scale mail. I also make handmade leather goods and have watercolour paintings, originals and prints. I sell these items online via Etsy and travel western Canada to large events like festivals and comic expos, meeting a variety of people and practicing continual learning and growth.

It was around the time I moved to the Kootenays that I really began to seriously study the runes and make them a daily practice, though I had dabbled a little before. I found that dabbling was never enough to really begin to digest the true wisdom, so this phase is when I would say I actually *learned* runes. With this study, I also became a member of the Asatru Community and spent time reading the *Eddas* and whatever else I could find on Norse mythology. My group of friends got me interested in tarot and Kabbalah again, after I had somewhat set it aside when studying the sciences. There is something super mystical about the region I live in that attracts mystical and occult folks. Some say it is because of leylines and crystals in the mountains. The fact that much of the geography is named after Norse mythos (the town of Ymir, the Valhalla mountain range, Mt. Loki, etc.) has made me feel quite at home, and I would say it makes a suitable place to practice paganism.

The literature on runes and Norse mythology is vast, and I would be lying if I told you I have read all of it, nor am I an expert in their history. I certainly have not read all the books, though I feel that after amalgamating the five or so sources of the runes I did read, along with the *Eddas*, I have developed a strong foundation. Now, upon writing this book, I have spent at least two years without reading a book on runes (though I still read Norse mythos, such as *The Saga of the Volsungs*), allowing myself to develop my own relationship with the runes, one that is exempt from the impressions of others. I have referenced the books and studies that came before me, but I only accessed them again after doing my writing and paintings without the influence of what others have written.

This biography should impress upon you that my background is diverse, and I am writing about the runes from both a scientific and intuitive spiritual perspective. I'm not the best at anything, I'm not the best artist, I'm certainly not a highly revered shaman, nor am I the most scholarly historian. As such, I won't pretend that I am, and my account might not be as detailed as the books written by those who truly are shamans or historians, but I would rather not just repeat their works and, instead, focus on creating my own.

I do feel, however, that I've been guided to create this book. My life tends to be driven by extreme levels of luck, both good and bad, where often the bad luck is what pushes me into a place of good. It was bad luck to not finish my MSc because of a poor choice in professor, but it was good luck to end up in the Kootenays and get to make my life as an artist work for me. It was bad luck that, in 2020, COVID-19 hit, and my usual festival circuit was disrupted, but it was good luck that it provided me the time necessary to do the art and writing to put this book together.

In these times and circumstances, I feel as though I have been guided, by Odin, by my spirit guides, by the universe, or by my own strange intuition. You can view it as you will. Whatever you name the force, I will acknowledge it and give thanks. I hope whatever force has driven me into creating this book also blesses you with some wisdom and knowledge as well.

The Art and Myth

This book is uniquely from my perspective, but the main purpose and intrigue is in the artwork. My painting style is something that I have developed since I was a teenager and first applied paint to canvas. Watercolour was only something that I practiced in late university, around the same time as truly learning the runes. I picked up a book called *Dreamscapes Myth & Magic* that teaches watercolour fantasy techniques, and then spent years after developing my own style.

The runes, being visual symbols, can be easily learned through visual cues. The symbols the runes represent are valuable information that can be understood without the use of words. This is closer to the vibrational meaning of the runes than a description. If you look at Fehu (ᚠ) and see a cow with its two horns, you can do the work yourself to understand what the meaning of the rune is. Each rune is best understood by looking at Nordic history, so the words I write are also powerful, but the method of teaching through imagery is a useful tool to aiding memory.

There are a number of decks of well illustrated rune cards that already exist to give visual aide to the runes. I, personally, do not use cards in my rune practice. I feel that the runes are at their most potent through the energies of chaos and random effects, and thus should be inscribed upon wood, bone or stone and cast on a cloth as they were historically used (see the section on Using the Runes for more information). This book is thus meant as a tool for someone to learn the runes with the runes in hand, so that they can work with the chaos that is their nature. However, I acknowledge that everyone's magickal practice is a personal journey, so if you use another method and find it works better for you, by all means, please use it and also enjoy this book.

Another aspect of this book that is a bit different from the ones that have come before it is my comparisons to other esoteric systems. Because of my time spent studying other systems, I have seen their wisdom and I will point out relevant aspects when I feel it is useful. This is meant to show the universality of these concepts, as well as make the runes easier to understand for people who have studied these more common systems. I understand Asatru and the runes are not the path for everyone, but hopefully with this book, people who practice other belief systems can also see the wisdom in the Asatru path by helping show our commonalities. And those who study Asatru can hopefully see our shared interest with other magickal practitioners, so we can create a larger community together.

I've also spent time learning about the hero's journey in the works of Joseph Campbell, which describes similarities in mythos among all of earth's cultures and relates this to our own psychology. The short of it is that we use fantasy and myth to understand not just extrinsic forces, but for understanding ourselves and our psyche. To study myth and religion is thus synonymous with studying oneself and is a powerful tool for individual growth.

Shamanism is very relevant in understanding the runes and Norse mythos. The word shaman is rooted in Siberian culture, but has since been used, sometimes controversially, as a general term for healers and guides of indigenous cultures who have travelled into the spirit realm to do their work. Shamanism, as a general practice, is well known to have been practiced in Siberia, South American and African cultures (sometimes under the influence of psychoactive substances) but was also performed by most ancient cultures, including the Germanic and Norse peoples before the spread of bigger religions. The purpose of the shaman was as a spiritual leader and healer, who would commune with spirits and gods. They would enter a trance, sometimes induced by music, to transfer their consciousness to another plane of reality, in which they could learn things that would be reported back into this reality. A good thing to keep in mind with shamanism is not to spend much time questioning if these experiences are real or not, because they did not occur in the physical reality in which we are most often conscious. They were real to the shaman experiencing them, they were real in the reality (such as the dream world) that they occurred in, and they gave real world benefits, even if these benefits were largely psychological.

One major theme in worldwide shamanism is the presence of the world tree. In Norse it is known as Yggdrasil, in India as Kalpa Vriksha Tree and in Mesoamerican cultures the *axis mundi*. The world tree also appears across Siberian, Roman, Chinese, Native American and South American mythos'. When I travelled to Peru, I encountered their tree of life and the animals that represent the branches, trunk and roots, which are the condor, jaguar and snake respectively. The importance is that it holds all the realms – the other worlds, together with ours. Simultaneously, humans all over the world have recognized that our position in the tree of life is at the center, the trunk, Midgard. The branches then hold up the realms of the gods and higher consciousness, and the roots are the place of connection to source energy and animal spirits.

This is where there is some connection to the Jewish Kabbalah system. There are ten sephira on their tree of life, spheres that represent different mental states that can be represented by gods of many cultures. This system did a great job of incorporating the mythos of Egypt, India, Biblical angels and Greece, and even Norse gods have some similarities to it. The days of the week, which have Germanic names related to Germanic gods, are related to different planets, or Roman gods, and this makes for a too-easy fit when it comes to Kabbalah that I don't think works well. Kabbalah can be used in tandem with the ideas of Joseph Campbell in understanding our psyche. However, the base sephiroth is that of our present physical realm, and the rest of the sephira, only represent the higher realms and forms of consciousness. The roots of the tree of life are not drawn. When the roots are included, they are seen as a mirror of the tree, which represents demons and darkness, highlighting the Jewish and Christian disconnection with natural forces. So, although Kabbalah is a valuable tool of modern magick, it focuses solely on connection with our gods and may be correlated to how humanity has become so disconnected from our planet.

It is thanks to modern technology and widespread education that we are able to take a step back and see the bigger picture of how myths have many commonalities among different cultures. There are many things to be thankful for in this age of knowledge, despite our disconnection from nature. Finding commonalities with other cultures and religions has stopped most religious wars that have been present for much of human history. No single system has all the answers, and no culture is immune to the demons that all human psyche is subject to. When we see that other people's demons bear the same face as our own, we no longer view the people as the demons, and it makes going to war a much more difficult task.

I know there are many followers of Odin who do not feel the same way and think that because the Aryan race can be seen to be blessed by the Norse gods, that they are supreme. But there are many ways we can dissolve this fallacy.

The first is by looking at the stories of Odin himself. Odin has one eye because he sacrificed the other to Mimir to drink from his well of knowledge. Mimir was a jotun, the giant race who were mortal enemies of the Aesir gods, but Odin still saw Mimir as an equal. The same applies to the jotun Loki who was Odin's blood brother. Odin also valued the knowledge of the Vanir, a different race of gods, and learned their ways through Freya. The Aesir often asked for help from the gnomes or dwarves, who had repulsive traits but were also valuable for their skill as smiths. Thusly, the gods saw value in many different species of humanoids, and it is hard to see how they would only value one skin colour of humans. Odin teaches travelling and gaining knowledge from many different people and perspectives, and true followers of Odin would be wise to listen to this lesson.

So, the runes are for everyone who wants to connect with Odin and the other Norse gods, not just people of European descent. However, you will likely find you are most connected to magick and gods of your own heritage, so people most likely to use the runes and connect with the Aesir and Vanir are those with Germanic heritage. It is also much easier to learn the runes if your native language is Germanic, including English. This is not exclusive though. Just as anyone from any race or religion can study yoga and benefit from its practice, so too can other races learn from the Elder Futhark. Please do not be afraid to learn about the runes if your heritage is not European.

The runes are a Germanic system because of their origin, which cannot be removed from the runes and is important for their understanding. I will be using Norse myths in my explanations of the runes, but please understand that when I mention Odin, Tyr or Thor, these gods may also be present by another name and face in any other belief system that someone may have. This doesn't mean one should try to use another pantheon, such as Egyptian or Chinese deities with the runes, as the Germanic gods are embedded in the Elder Futhark and the Futhark are an alphabet that allows one to connect and commune with them. Chinese letters and Egyptian hieroglyphs belong with their gods and stories, just as the runes belong with the Norse.

There is one other aspect of mysticism, manifestation, that I should explain because I mention it within the runes on multiple occasions. Manifestation is essentially the use of willpower to bend reality. I once did a spoon bending workshop, in which we drew upon source and sky energy to bend spoons. On my second and third tries, the spoons I had brought that I could not normally bend without extreme force twisted under my hands in a spiral, as though the metal was as soft as butter. The primary force that was used to bend the spoons was my mind, my belief, and the calling of spirit energy from the other realms that I am connected to. I had to first acknowledge the doubt and disbelief that spoon bending was physically possible, then let it go and let the force flow. Manifestation works the same way, where you can imagine things into reality by applying energy and willpower, then stepping back and letting the universe flow. I once heard the story of a millionaire actor who, when he was poor, had written himself a fake cheque for one million dollars for acting services. Years later he got to cash in on the real thing. But manifestation isn't just about writing yourself a fake cheque, this actor also spent years of his life dedicated to his trade and put in effort and hard work. The manifestation tool helped to keep him on the right track, but he also put in the energy necessary to make that manifestation become reality.

Our minds are powerful tools, and runes are a type of key that can be used for manifestation and other magickal workings. Magick is a construct of the mind, a tool if you will, and is only as powerful as the mind that applies it. Magick, at its foremost, taps into our subconscious and helps us master our psyche. It takes a certain level of faith to use any kind of magick, as you have to balance doubts and reality with tapping into those energies and forces that don't exist within the physical, tangible, explainable, scientific realm. But as with most ways of thinking, the mind can be trained, and the more you practice, the stronger the tool it will be. The more you practice runes, the stronger your rune magick will be. The more you honour your connection to your gods and the universe, the more you can channel their arcane energies.

So, before you dive into these runes, I ask you to take a step back to check your perspective. Are you skeptical of their use? Are you excited, with no doubts in your mind whatsoever? Are you ready to practice them, and learn more about yourself and your psyche? Or, are you simply interested in looking at the pretty pictures I have painted? There are no wrong answers but be honest with yourself. You don't need to put the runes into practice to gain something from this book. I don't think the runes are the end-all answer to everything, nor are they for everyone. But they are potent magick. Should you use them, regular mental checks will help you stay grounded and get more out of your practice.

OTHER NOTES

IN WRITING THIS BOOK, I CHOSE TO FOCUS ON THE IMAGES THE RUNES ARE MEANT TO SYMBOLIZE, E.G. Fehu (ᚠ) and the cow. But around the cow, there are also images of grapes and apples, which are additional symbols of abundance. There are many hidden symbols like these in each of the paintings of the runes, and I will explain many, but the more time you spend looking them the more images you will surely notice. I also try to incorporate the rune shape in some of the background images, like Kenaz (ᚲ) and how the sparks are shaped like the rune.

I chose the colours of the runes based on how I see them. Most often these colour associations also relate to the element of the rune, such as how Berkano is an earth rune and therefore green, Laguz is blue for water, Kenaz orange for fire and Mannaz a tan colour for air. There might be people who have more thoughtful colour associations, but I am going off my own personal relationship with the runes. I have synaesthesia, so English letters typically have colours and my rune associations sometimes align with these. For example, I see the letter O as black, which is the same colour I envision Othala.

I chose to draw all of the runes using 3 as a base number. All of the rune drawings, therefore, have been completed using a consistent 18 cm height, with all other aspects being placed at drafted 60° positions, and with lengths that were also multiples of 3, 6 or 9 wherever possible. On occasion these lines strayed somewhat if it seemed awkward artistically, but in general I used the grid of the web of Wyrd in sketching all of the runes. Sowilo is the exception and is the only one with a horizontal line, as I wanted to steer clear from the version of it that is used in the Swastika (see rune description).

I have also decided to choose words from the English language that contain the sounds the runes make that also convey some of the meaning of the rune. If you think back to what I mentioned of the kiki/bouba effect, you will realize that these sounds have some universal properties that are carried in every language. So English, even if the words do not come directly from its German roots, still carries the meaning of the runes in many of the words we use. So, the words I have chosen from English are simply examples of how the runes and the vibrations carry into our language and do not necessarily reflect similar German or Scandinavian words.

I've applied my own version of the hero's journey through the runes. It is not a reworking of Joseph Campbell's hero's journey, though it may bear some similarities. The runes are a cycle, and there are even cycles within the larger cycle, rather than a singular up and down journey like that of Joseph Campbell's hero. The runes give way to the next generation after Othala where our hero settles down and begin with the new in Fehu, where new life is created, beginning the cycle anew. My hero journey's main purpose is to provide some logic for the transition between one rune to the next within that cycle with the use of a story. I also explore the psychological aspects of the runes, which are entwined within the transitions, but the primary purpose is simply to illustrate the transitions to aid in learning.

The story of the hero is one that I began putting together years ago, as a way to explain the runes to students in a workshop I taught. It is now the story of one, but then I had told it as the creation story, where we began as matter and evolved through the first aett to the point where we built society in Wunjo. It was well received, if incomplete, and the students were eager to me to finish the story as it went through all of the runes. The hero's story is the result of those musings and my hope is that it will provide another layer of understanding to those who read it.

The runes are divided into three groups called aetts. Each aett consists of eight runes, which is why the runes are often seen arranged in three lines of eight. The beginning rune of each aett is said to correspond to a god or goddess with the particular rune sound at the beginning of their name. The first aett begins with the F rune, Fehu, and is that of Freya. Freya is an earth goddess and her aett is about physical evolution. The second aett begins with the H rune, Hagalaz, and is the aett of Heimdall. Heimdall is the watcher at the top of the rainbow bridge and his aett is an inward journey of self development. The final aett begins with the T rune Tiwaz and is the aett of Tyr. Tyr is the god of justice, and his aett is that of honour. There is a detailed summary of the gods and their aetts at the beginning of each.

Some runes have merkstave, or inverted positions. These don't represent what can be the complete opposite, but instead are polarities like two heads on the same coin. You cannot have life without death (both are principles of life), day without night (both aspects of time), or up without down (two aspects of direction). For each of those examples, the principle is the same, but each is a different aspect that can be seen as positive or negative. Merkstave position runes are something like the 'negative', the downsides of the runes. Merkstave can therefore highlight areas that need work, for example an inverted Kenaz is stifled creativity or the downside of creativity which is a burnout. But it is not the complete opposite of creation which would be destruction. Runes without a merkstave position are ones that do not have this duality aspect and have straightforward meanings. For example, Dagaz is not day or night but the point in between day and night and thus the transition point. It doesn't have a dark or a light side, because it is transition itself and the neutral middle between those two opposites.

Some of you might also notice I do not have the so called 'blank rune' in my writings. By definition, the rune is a sound. Some people might see the absence of sound as useful in divination, but this is a new age construct I don't personally use. The blank rune was originally just an extra piece given in the sets of 24 runes, as 25 is a nice squared number. The blank rune is most useful as an extra piece if you lose one of the 24 and need to carve yourself a replacement. Again, you might see some purpose in drawing this blank with your set of runes, and that's fine, but this paragraph is as much as I will write about it.

Freya's Aett

Freya is the Vanir goddess of love and of war (colloquially as "fucking & fighting" or "slaying & laying"). She is the beloved princess of the Vanir gods and is also admired and loved by all the Aesir. There are multiple stories of jotuns trying to find a way to goad the gods into giving them her hand in marriage. She was married to the god Odr (who is gone on a journey) for whom she mourns. Freya had two daughters with him. Despite her mourning, Freya is also known for her promiscuity, as she obtained her Brisingamen necklace by sleeping with the four dwarves that made it, and Loki accuses her as having slept with everyone (it is worth noting that this is everyone, not every man) in Aegir's hall during the feast after Baldur's death.

Fólkvangr ("field of the people") is Freya's domain, where she brings her half of the warriors who were slain in battle). She also accepts women who have died a noble death. Popular myth states that she is the Valkyrie queen, though this is a misinterpretation as the Valkyries, who gather the other half of the slain, are of Odin.

Freya is also the archetype of a powerful shaman known as a völva and is known for teaching the art of seidr magick to Odin. This was primarily a woman's form of magick and Odin is seen as somewhat lowering himself to learn it from her. She has a feathered cloak that she uses to transform into a falcon to fly between the worlds of Yggdrasil. This feathered cloak is part of her seidr magick, as being able to traverse the spirit realms is part of her magick, and the falcon is a spirit animal known for its speed and keen eyesight. She also gets around using a chariot pulled by cats, which were known to complete a family home by being guardians that kept out the evil rodents.

I've depicted Freya here wearing nothing except a helm of white feathers, to highlight her warrior aspect while portraying her seductive nature. At her neck is the gleaming golden Brisingamen pendant.

In summary, Freya is a goddess with many aspects such as love, war, magick, and fertility. They mostly convene around earthly matters, which is the lesson of the first aett of runes. It is the physical and material journey. This is the story of human evolution which begins with how we evolved from matter (Fehu) into beast (Uruz). The beast then created tools (Thurisaz) and advanced its mind, learned to speak, read and write (Ansuz) and left the wilderness (Raidho). We mastered fire and creation (Kenaz), learned harmony with others (Gebo) and built communities (Wunjo). Freya's aett teaches what we need to live as humans to meet our basic needs.

1. Fehu

[fay-hoo]: the phonetic 'f' sound, such as in fortune, food, full, fulfill, fruit, etc.

Fehu means "cattle" or "cow." Fehu and cattle represented wealth to the Norse. Wealth in more than just the monetary sense, but in the aspect of where you lived, what you ate and the air you breathed. In short, Fehu represents physical abundance and the transfer of matter between beings. When this rune comes up, it is a positive sign that you will receive and enjoy wealth in some form or another. The image of Fehu is that of a cow. The two lines upwards are the cow's two horns

Here the cow is docile and sweet. She is content in her being. Perhaps she knows her fate is at the hands of her master and is content in the knowledge that the purpose of her existence is to feed him. This may sound grim, but technically that is the purpose of all life, to feed something else. Or perhaps she is in ignorant bliss, as Fehu is about matter with little mind.

Fehu is one of the most straightforward runes. It is the transfer of energy known as the food web. This is the story of how matter is moved between beings to create life. This is what life is, this is the material world. The cow is its symbol because, to the Norse, this was a major resource for meat, milk, clothing, etc. The cows would eat the grass, the people (and their dogs) would eat the cows. The grass was fertilized by the waste and bodies left behind, and the cycle continued.

Scientifically, we now know that it is about atoms, which make up molecules, which make up living beings. The continual transfer of atoms is what keeps us alive. Life is atoms in motion. By eating, drinking or even breathing, we take up atoms from the environment and they become a part of our body. We then exhale or excrete those atoms, which are used by other life forms. Sometimes those life forms create chemicals that then become fuel for our bodies. Fehu, at its simplest, can be seen as an atom.

Fehu is a major earth rune, being that of matter. It also relates to physical abundance of any kind. This includes money and your home, but a person can also be wealthy in their food and surroundings. Being able to swim in mountain rivers, eat chocolate regularly, or breathe a clean ocean breeze are all forms of wealth that are contained in Fehu.

In the sequence of runes Fehu comes first, but it is also after Othala. Othala was the home and the hearth, and Fehu is the cattle around it. The home came first, and then this space of safety bred abundance and life, which we see in Fehu. Here Fehu may represent a new hero in babe form, undifferentiated and unhardened.

The apples represent the goddess Idunn's apples of youth. She tends these apples and gifts only bites to the gods as needed to maintain their agelessness. There is a story where Loki brings Idunn and her apples to the giant, Tjazi, after being tortured into the deed or tricked, depending on the story's version. The gods are then in dismay, as they quickly become old and grey without her. They eventually find this was Loki's doing and send him back to steal her, and her apples, from the giant. This highlights the value of apples, which were a prized and delicious fruit of the fall harvest. Apples fall in abundance off trees and was undoubtedly an important life-giving food for the old Norse.

Merkstave, Fehu represents hard times. It will often come on the days you find you cannot spend money the way you would like and are perhaps feeling anxious about how to bring abundance to your life. Now might be a good time to appreciate that which you do have and focus on other ways of fulfilling your desires.

2. Uruz

[oo-rooz]: the phonetic 'oo' sound, as in food or moo.[1]

Uruz means "aurochs," the extinct and untameable beast-cow. This rune relates to the heart of the beast, the indomitable will to live and thrive despite the odds. Like the windswept conifers at his feet, aurochs were built and meant for the freedom of the wild. They were stronger and had more character than the cows, and mystery because of it. Uruz is about powerful heart-space, the character that is developed from it and the strength and healing one can find when accessing it.

Where Fehu was loose, floating matter, here we now see matter manifested into a higher form. The loose atom, the animal that was meant for dinner, has now gained character and substance. The hero has been formed. The auroch could not be herded like cattle and was a source of mystery and awe. It was a hero in its own right.

Uruz allows you to find your center and tap into the survivor within. It's not just a survivor, but a fighter, not just dealing with strife but thriving in it. This rune can aid in healing and health for those who are sick, allowing one to thrive and flourish despite the odds. It can also aid in using traumas to create better versions of yourself. With Uruz, your scars can be wielded like trophies.

One should not focus on the strife aspect of Uruz, as strife will be presented later in Hagalaz. Nor is Uruz about the endurance of Isa that relates more to a pause and escape. Instead, the message is about the thriving, head-on strength aspect needed to take on challenges.

There is also a magickal aspect of manifestation in this rune that should be noted. Its shape, although somewhat auroch-like, has been said to represent the initial, upward draw of energy from its source, which is then given direction and released back.

---

1. It is used more commonly in German words like Blüt, meaning blood.

It is for this, and the heart-related aspect, that I chose to represent this rune in purple (it should perhaps be more of a pink/purple, but the stylish blue suited the landscape better). I wanted to make sure ice was incorporated, despite this being an earthy rune. This relates to the original cow, Audumla, who licked the ice of Niflheim to provide milk to the frost giant, Ymir, who birthed all life thereafter, and whose body became the world.

The bent bristlecones are a naturally bonsaied tree, again representing beauty and unique strength, appearing and creating a thriving life despite the forces against them. They are tiny but ancient trees that have survived many seasons and trials, unlike many that share this harsh environment.

The merkstave position of this rune represents a lack of strength or health. It is saying you haven't been paying attention to your body and are not in your place of power. Take time to tune in. Pay attention and be slow and deliberate in your life choices; make decisions you can feel good about in the future.

3. Thurisaz

[thoo-ree-sahz]: the phonetic 'th' sound, such as in thorn, thing, or thrust.

Thurisaz - Thur - Thor. The thorn, Mjolnir, the giant. Thurisaz is about the god of thunder, Thor, who wielded his mighty hammer Mjolnir in countless battles against the giants, the jotuns. He was the thorn in their side, the adversary, the slayer of jotuns.

Thurisaz is distinctly related to Mars in its destructive powers. Thurisaz is a double-edged sword, one that can be used as a weapon to break down barriers and allow you to slay giants, but you will often have a price to pay. Directionality is particularly important in this rune, to ensure the destructive force is wielded upon the intentional recipient.

It is a mighty and powerful rune, used to bust through whatever may be holding you back. It is a tool that can be used for forward progress. It is wisely used when one feels a sense of stagnation or being trapped. Your problems may appear to be overwhelming giants, but there is a tool waiting to be found to allow you to rise above and beyond them.

Fehu began with matter, then in Uruz it was given character and independence. In Thurisaz our hero has found his sword, his hammer, or his bow, whatever he needs to not just endure the forces of nature but shape it to the future he wants to see. Thurisaz may be any tool that can be applied to any problem. These problems may appear as giants, but you are equipped with the weapons you need to slay them.

The image of Thurisaz is often considered to be Mjolnir, but it also appears to be a thorn. It is referred to as a thorn in the Anglo-Saxon rune poem. A thorn is a symbol of pain and the weapon of the rose. The rose is an important symbol, not just for the painful thorn, but for the message that there is a reward for the pain endured.

The thorn is also a symbol of defence. Thor was the defender of Asgard, a strong and reliable figure. He was said to come to the aid of anyone who was in need and would defend Asgard whenever summoned. He was also the defender of the common castes in Norse society and represented their patron deity, thus why many Asatruar wear a Mjolnir pendant.

The Mars force, and that of Thurisaz, is that of the masculine fire. It can be applied creatively or destructively. Its main aspect is drive and applied force. One symbol of Thurisaz is that of a phallus, representing this male energy, while doubling as that of a 'tool.' Mars is as much about drive as it is destruction, and the phallus is the representation of male sexuality, that of the drive. Even in women, our sexual desires are fuelled by testosterone, which is masculine in nature.

The demon depicted is a rendition of Surtr, the fire jotun born of Muspelheim who comes at Ragnarok. Though Surtr's fate is linked with Freyr, and Thor with Jörmundangr (the serpent that encircles the world), I chose to stylistically include Thor and Surtr together for this rune, to better portray the fiery Mars aspect.

Thurisaz links very closely to pain and becomes directed at the self in the merkstave position. I find it often comes up merkstave during menstrual cycles or hangovers. It can be merkstave in a reading to you if you are misdirecting destructive energies, which should be left for slaying giants and not harming those close to you.

4. Ansuz

[ahn-sooz]: *the phonetic short 'ah' sound, such as in answer[2], amaze or above.*

Ansuz means "answer." Words, communication, language, music and divine messages all give a gentle and brief summary of this rune. It is an airy and fleeting rune that is a little less tangible and may be harder to grasp. This rune represents the question and, simultaneously, the answer. It is primarily the rune of sound, speech, words and communication.

Our nameless hero found his tool in Thurisaz, but in Ansuz he finds his purpose. He looks to the sky and asks the gods for an answer. In return he is given his reason. The man who chose the sword becomes a warrior, the man with a harpoon becomes a fisherman, the man with a hammer a blacksmith. We now understand not how to use the tool but *why*.

The image is of the windswept cloak of Odin, the All-Father. It is to Odin not only the Norse, but also their pantheon of the Aesir, turned to for answers because of his depth of knowledge. In one story, he sacrificed his right eye to gain knowledge at Mimir's well. He hung upside down for nine days and nine nights after sacrificing himself on his spear to gain the knowledge of the runes in another. Lastly, he learned seidr, the ancient earth magick, from Freya. He is not just a master warrior in Valhalla, training warriors for Ragnarok, but also a wise wizard.

Odin often appears to people as a wanderer with a walking stick, humbling himself as he walks among us, learning of us, telling tales and asking questions in a quest to gain and teach knowledge. There is a link to Odin's wandering nature and the high importance that the Norse place on hospitality, particularly to travelling strangers. There is a theory that Odin was really an ancient shaman, so powerful that the stories eventually morphed him into a god figure.

---

2. The short 'a' is prounced differently depending on the dialect, but the Germanic root is a distinct 'ah' sound.

Above him fly Hugin and Munin, representing thought and memory/mind, respectively. Daily they would fly out and bring Odin knowledge of what happens on Midgard. Thusly, ravens were also highly revered. In the *Poetic Edda* it is stated that Odin fears they may not return. He fears for Hugin, but more for Munin, reflective of the importance of keeping oneself even if thought is lost.

Ansuz is everywhere and nowhere. Unless a one-eyed stranger knocks on your door, you must find it in the smaller things, such as the wise words of a stranger, an animal that crosses your path, meditation and breath work, the sense of harmony and connectedness that comes with dance and music, or an "I love you" from a loved one. The moments and feelings are fleeting and cannot be held on to, but they last a lifetime. To experience and master the secrets of Ansuz is the key to divine ecstasy. It is ever moving, but always there for those who seek higher knowledge and purpose.

Ansuz merkstave says you have not been paying attention to your purpose. There is a disconnect with your gods, and you may be feeling like there is no purpose or answer. Now is a good time to meditate, pray, go on a vision quest or whatever way you connect with higher powers. If you are a not a pious person you can still find that connection in simple acts of writing, poetry, dance or song.

5. Raidho

[rah-ee-doh]: the phonetic 'r' sound, as found in ride, run, rhythm or race.

To ride is the heart of Raidho. Thor's chariot, or that of Sol as she rides across the sky every day. This is the rune of the traveler that is used to give protection and forward motion in life and on journeys. It relates to rhythm and dance, where Ansuz was the sound, we now have a beat we can move to.

The Germanic deity of Sol is one of the few instances from the ancient world where the sun is represented as female. She rides a chariot across the sky, drawn by two horses, Arvakr and Alsvidr. Her brother Mani, the moon, and she are pursued by the wolves Skoll and Hati in eternal motion through the skies.

The Sol link to Raidho seems the most important to me, but Thor should also be mentioned in this rune. Thor also rides a chariot pulled by two goats that he can slaughter, eat and resurrect to continue his adventures. He travels often, and adventure is a large part of his stories.

One must also clarify at this point that this rune does not represent the sun itself, which is found in the rune Sowilo, but the path which it takes and the motion that carries it forward. It is also representative of the planet's position to the sun and the perpetual motion that is part of life.

Raidho also represents movement from one stage of initiation to the next, the steps in one's journey. It is relevant for students, and those looking for work advancement, to move homes or leave a stagnant relationship, for the obvious travel aspect. This rune places importance on the order and progression of endeavours like education and ritual, where progress is unidirectional and intentional.

Here we see our hero riding forth from her place of safety, armed with nothing but her weapon (Thurisaz) and purpose (Ansuz). Two ravens circle the castle, representing Odin's presence encouraging her on her way. The road is well-travelled and laid out; she is sure of herself and the route she is taking. Her horse is her chariot, her mount, her way forward.

This image has a lot more elements to it than the four previous ones, despite the rather simple meaning. The mountain can be taken to represent a slain giant, the castle safety, the wheel motion, the chariot the vessel, the path the route, etc. The journey is often best explained not by one static symbol, but in a larger story.

The rune itself is meant to be an image of a chariot. The image here is not overlaid, and with Raidho it can be hard to picture how the symbol is a chariot. But if you imagine the equilateral triangle as a wheel, you can see how the lines represent handles and a place to stand, respectively. I've also seen it drawn where the wheel is the part below, and the triangle on top is that of the person standing.

Merkstave, Raidho generally represents a lack of change. Perhaps you have been in one place too long, or you haven't been putting in the preparations you need to make the next step in whatever it is you are trying to accomplish. Find where the blockage is, take the time to dismantle it and free your energy to continue moving forward. Another interpretation could be a journey gone wrong, or in the wrong direction.

6. Kenaz

[ken-ahz]: the phonetic 'k' sound, like in create, carry, or carve.

The forge's fire, "the torch." The sparks struck from Thor's anvil. This rune at its most basic speaks of the inner spark of creativity. It is the drive to make and create, to forge something into something else via alchemy. Where Thurisaz was the destructive Mars force, we see this channelled into positive creative energy in Kenaz. Kenaz is about being the light to inspire others and acting as a beacon.

This rune is as much about the small, fleeting momentary spark of inspiration as it is about repetition and mastery of skill. This repetition is known as temperance. The more you hone the skill and make yourself work towards something every day, the easier it will be to find that creative spark and will to be the maker of something. Sometimes it isn't there, which is the merkstave representation of Kenaz, and that is okay too (fiery energy is about high highs and low lows), but part of mastery is riding those waves and learning to control and use them to your advantage. But it begins with the spark, and one should always find an outlet when the drive and desire is there to create.

If we continue the story of our hero, they journeyed forth in Raidho, with tool (Thurisaz) and purpose (Ansuz), and in Kenaz they are now putting both to use. The hammer we found in Thurisaz is now being used to forge and create, after having slain the giants that were causing us grief.

As most creative folks know, inspiration often comes through channels outside of oneself. You have to leave your comfort zone to find new ground and truly become a master of what it is you do. In doing so, you will also inspire others! See the next few runes for how this plays out but think now on the torch meaning. By being the light, doing your best and shining your brightest, you can light the way for others.

The spark is also a sexual innuendo. It is that initial hot phase, the feel of the flare in your loins, the drive for pleasure and to create passion. This can be channelled many ways, but the basis is that this rune can be used to help create that initial spark. It is then up to you to create a foundation or a hearth to keep that flame burning if you so wish.

Alchemy is also an important concept here. It relates to the change of the metal being hammered into a sword, on the principle that matter can neither be created nor destroyed, only changed. But it also speaks to the inner changes: the transformation, regeneration and sacrifice that happens in the pursuit of mastery. This rune carries with it the fiery energy of the phoenix or the dragon, both mythical beasts of transformation.

There is also a healing aspect to Kenaz. Think of art therapy and the regenerative effects creation can have. Art truly can be like a healing flame, allowing folks to release and temper those inner demons into something thriving and beautiful. The torch is a light. It can be used as a beacon to show the way for others.

If you have received a merkstave Kenaz in your reading, you may not be feeling the most creative, but this rune is telling you to not give up. You may feel your light has gone out and you are not in your place of power, but fear not, there will be other days. This burnout is the downside of creativity, as you will not be maximally inspired every day.

7. Gebo

[gay-boh]: the phonetic 'g' sound, as in gift, great or good.

Gebo means "the gift" or "generosity." Giving and receiving. This is a harmonious rune representing a balanced exchange of energy between two poles.

Gebo I see as a watery rune, full of juicy energy and emotion. It is the rune of the lovers, showing the moment that two have become one. Their life force is bonded as they give all of themselves in an act of trust and reciprocity.

In Kenaz, a spark was created. Our hero picked up the torch and became the light, a glowing and expressive version of themselves. And in Gebo, that energy and drive is now shared. Not only can we offer our energy to another, but the beauty that is us has attracted another who wants to give and show us their light in turn. And so, two become one, and the light created together is greater than the torches held alone.

The image of Gebo is straightforward, that of two humans connected at the hips. I have also seen it depicted as kissing lips. This rune is useful for sex magick and attracting a lover.

Gebo has symmetry above and below, as well as from side to side. This acknowledges the balance of right and left (masculine and feminine) and above and below (divine and mundane) energetic exchanges. Gebo is also a representation of mind/spirit and body linked together. Then we give to another, be it to a mortal or a god, we receive a blessing in return, and the whole creates a picture that is greater than the sum of its parts.

We must acknowledge the divine gifts we receive and do our part to maintain the balance. We must be honest and caring lovers to be fair to our partner, we should give gifts to those who have helped us in the past, and so must we be grateful to the

gods when they have bestowed fortune upon us. Give thanks for that which you have received. Give offerings in whatever way you can. Do not expect to receive if you are not also willing to give.

I find this rune is often drawn on days when I spend time with my son. Our family and our children are very important gifts that should never be forgotten. And the more we find time and love for them, the more that energy is reciprocated back, sometimes in ways you might not even imagine.

Gebo is the first of the runes with no merkstave position, when this rune is upside down it is the same as right side up. This symmetry represents the most balanced runes, the ones in which there is no repressed or negative side. Giving should always be balanced and reciprocal, and there is no negative way in which to gift. Keep in mind, however, as this is the rune of reciprocity, the message that "you get what you give" applies to harmful 'gifts' as well. If what you give out into the world are thoughts of spite and malice, expect to have that energy returned in like.

8. Wunjo

[vun-joh]: the phonetic 'v' sound in English, or 'w' in Germanic languages.[3]

WUNJO MEANS JOY! Community, connection and celebration are all major themes in this rune. It is the joy found in time spent with others, and the feeling of solidarity in working together for a common cause.

Wunjo is something of a respite before the next three more challenging runes. I recommend you rest here and enjoy before moving forward. Wunjo is the reward for the hard work spent through Freya's Aett, think of it as Freya's gift if you will. It is the result of not just one person's spark, like in Kenaz, or the shared gift of two balanced sparks in Gebo, but now a whole tribe of sparkling humans whose roads have converged and all share their gifts in a big, thriving network.

The best part of community is the diversity. Everyone's tool (Thurisaz), purpose (Ansuz), and journey (Raidho) are as unique as each individual. But here they have all come together in balance and harmony and joy to share their skills and gifts in a bigger, joyous entity that is greater than each individual part. This is the power of synergy, where the whole is significantly more than the sum of all parts.

Think of how a roadside blacksmith wouldn't succeed unless he had farmers around as well. Or how, when there are people that specialize in farming, it allows others to focus on things like science and medicine. Humans do not thrive individually. We must find our individuality to be able to contribute to society, but to be the best versions of ourselves we must all work together.

To come together and thrive we need something to unite us. This is Wunjo. The image of Wunjo is a flag. The flag is a symbol that unites people. Symbols can transcend words in their ability to convey meaning and purpose, and when it is raised on a pole for all to see, it draws people of similar value and like-mindedness. It gives

---

3. 'w' is pronounced like a 'v' in Germanic languages, this sound exists in world (German "Welt" pronounced like 'V'elt), wish (Germanic wünschen), and wonder (German Wunder).

us purpose outside of our own individual purpose and journey. It can even allow us to look past the traits of people we don't necessarily like or agree with to create a working relationship, because we know that our community is better off with them also bringing their light.

The village in the painting purposely includes a diverse array of individuals. It has the very young to the very old, both of which are important in providing a holistic view of the world and contributing to a whole society. The village may be that of a historic Nordic village, but the people are more like that of today, where many types of people are dancing together. In Wunjo we are connected by a purpose that is larger than that of our individual consciousnesses, and we celebrate together in this moment regardless of other factors, such as age, societal standing or race.

The hummingbird is not native to Europe, but it is a universal animal symbol for joy, and here it is pollinating a honeysuckle. Honeysuckle also conveys innocence, joy, summer, and the festive energy that is Wunjo. These two organisms exist in a symbiotic relationship, where the hummingbird is provided food, and the flower gets to spread its pollen. Neither could exist without the other, both have existed for many millennia because of the perfect harmony that exists between the two. So not only is each its own representation of joy, but the symbiosis between the two is the primary message in Wunjo.

Other symbolic images are in this painting that are meant to help convey the message of Wunjo. One is the bonfire, which has always been a connecting source for humans as a safe and warm space. Another is the maypole, where the young folk dance around merrily in celebration of the coming summer. The crossroads show that there is more than one path that has led people to this community.

This rune almost always comes up for me during festival season. It is Wunjo at its finest, where you can find happy hippies next to lawyers doing yoga and dancing and drinking together. The music, in this case, brings people together who may never speak in other circumstances to celebrate something they find common ground in. Another time I experience this rune is when either I need to reach out for help, for something like moving my home, or when I am able to be there and provide the help someone else in my community needs.

Overall, the meaning of this rune is true joy. It is not just a single ecstatic experience, but a larger purpose that keeps us going and gives us meaning while also holding us in hard times. It gives us connection and celebration and reminds us that there is so much in this life worth celebrating.

Merkstave, this rune represents a lack of community. It can mean feeling disconnected, not having your place in society, or not participating in your community in a way that is meaningful. If this rune appears to you merkstave, you may want to seek out community by finding a way to contribute to it.

Heimdall's Aett

HEIMDALL REPRESENTS THE SECOND AETT. Heimdall is the god who stands guard on the end of the rainbow bridge, Bifröst . He bears the Gjallarhorn, the horn which is blown to warn of intruders and heralds Ragnarok. He is the brightest Aesir, with golden teeth and far seeing eyes. He is Loki's mortal enemy and combats him as a seal to return Freya's Brisingamen pendant. He is said to have taught the runes to humans and brought the three social classes that the Norse adhered to.

Heimdall is said to have nine jotun mothers and Odin as his father. One theory is that the mothers are the nine daughters of the sea gods Aegir and Ran, which would make Heimdall birthed of the sea. Similar to how Thor was born of mother earth and father sky, this would make Heimdall of the ocean and the sky. However, the names of his mothers don't fit this tale and so it is only just a theory.

Heimdall has a hall at the edge of Asgard, named Himinbjög (heaven's mountain) that is praised by Odin as one of the loveliest places in Asgard. It is located at the top of the rainbow bridge, where Heimdall fulfills his duty as watchman while enjoying an abundant Aesir lifestyle, drinking fine mead. He rides the golden maned horse Gulltoppr. This quality of hall, life, and horse are symbols of Heimdall's high status within the Norse pantheon, relative to his role as watchman and gatekeeper.

I've painted Heimdall as pale and blonde, as he is described in the Eddas. I used a blue tint to his shadows to represent him being birthed of the sea despite the questionability of the tale. The ram is said to be a totem of Heimdall (along with the rooster). His helmet has ram's horns and an embellishment on the third eye for his far-seeing nature. The Gjallarhorn curves over his shoulder, ready to signal the end of days.

Heimdall's aett is often seen as the most difficult sequence of runes. It is a journey that takes us inwards, it shakes our reality and makes us leave our safety to renew ourselves. This aett begins with destruction in Hagalaz, removing us from the joyful community we founded in Wunjo. Hagalaz, Nauthiz and Isa are known as the three Norns and symbolize various states of trauma, or past, present and future. The rest of the aett finds us learning to move onwards with life, culminating in Sowilo, representing success. The major theme to keep in mind is that this is an internal, mental journey that challenges us to grow as individuals.

9. Hagalaz

[hah-gah-lahz]: the phonetic 'h' sound, as in hail, hate, heart, health and harmony.

Hagalaz means "hail." The snowflake. The cosmic egg. This rune represents sudden, unrelenting and unstoppable disruption, and the opportunity that follows such. It is often regarded as the most powerful and important rune, as well as containing the most depth of wisdom. Thusly, it requires a great deal of reflection to grasp the full meaning. It should never be invoked lightly.

Starting its destructive aspect, Hagalaz leads directly after Wunjo, which represents the joy and community finally formed. Hagalaz can be one of many forces, be it hail that comes and destroys the crops, a large fire that burns down all the homes, or a disease that sweeps through and kills many. It is a force of nature that comes unexpectedly out of nowhere, taking away the happiness and the safety of everything we have spent so much energy to bring together. In its most overwhelming, it takes away our sense of purpose and everything we thought was true. It may also signify a relationship break up, quitting one's job, a car accident or an epiphany.

But do not despair! If this is upsetting or feels too intense, flip back to Uruz. Indeed, Uruz, your heart and your strength, may be what helps you to get through this difficult rune; it is the only thing that Hagalaz cannot take from you. Not everyone dies. There is a seed left to regrow crops, and out there somewhere is a new place to set up home and community. This trial is meant to bring you back into yourself to focus on that heart space and temper you into becoming a stronger individual.

This rune is the first of the three Norns, the three women who spin the fates of all mankind. They live at the base of Yggdrasil and water its roots. When a child is born, their fate is woven by Urd, Verdandi and then Skuld. Urd or Urth (Urðr), the spinner of the past, is said to represent Hagalaz. The message is that everything we

have done in the past has led us up to this point. That which we have built had flaws, and Hagalaz/Urd is making us aware of our mortality and the fragility of what seemed so perfect only moments before. It is now time to put what we had into the past also.

Urd is sometimes also Wyrd (pronounced like weird) and represents the web of Wyrd. The web of Wyrd is drawn as a repeating pattern of isometric triangles, and if you take six Hagalaz and overlay them you can create this symbol. It is the infinite cosmos from which all else is created. It is from this web of fate that our pattern is first drawn. Ultimately, it is a combination of the past, present and future that all three Norns use in creating the fate of a newborn.

Perhaps now you may begin to see Hagalaz is not just an end, but also a new beginning. The web of Wyrd, the repeating pattern of 60° triangles is that from which all other runes are created. Every rune is some combination of parts of these triangles. The web of Wyrd is not just the fabric from which we are created, but of everything in the universe. The destruction Hagalaz wrought may have taken away all that we knew, perhaps tore away the very fabric of reality, but once the veil is removed, what we are left with is infinite possibility. This is the important message of this powerful rune; it may not be for the faint of heart but if you have the strength to take Hagalaz head on you will find you can manifest anything into reality.

The image of the traditional Elder Futhark Hagalaz doesn't look like much on its own. It can be overlapped to create the web of Wyrd, as mentioned, and it is something like how the 'h' sound is formed by our mouths. It also has the benefit of looking like something of a bindrune of two Uruz (one upside down on top of another), which again shows the relationship between these two runes. But if you want a better representative image, I think the snowflake form found in the Younger Futhark and Armanen runes makes more sense intuitively as it directly looks like the web of Wyrd. The snowflake form of the rune is in the background of this image, so one may use it for reflection and study as well as the traditional Elder Futhark forefront 'h' form.

Neither form of this rune has a merkstave position. And though there is an aspect of chaos as well as order that comes with Hagalaz, both forces come together in harmony. It says you will not receive a chaotic destruction without also being given opportunity for new growth, and you will not receive that gift of infinite possibility without destruction.

The snowflake Hagalaz represents the seed, or cosmic egg, of Ymir, the frost giant at the beginning of time who was fed by Audumla (again referring back to Uruz). Hagalaz is an icy frost rune and is representative of Niflheim, the world of ice. But one should not ignore the fire aspect of Muspelheim that is contained in Hagalaz, as it was the other world present at the beginning of creation and life could not be created by one without the other. The Tower card in tarot has the same aspects as Hagalaz and is represented as fire. Ymir and Audumla were both born by the interaction of Niflheim and Muspelheim, and these two forces were from which all creation came, including the Norns. So, Hagalaz is simultaneously both realms. There is a duality aspect in Hagalaz that is universal, not only in the fire vs ice aspect, but between destruction and creation.

Refer to Robert Frost's infamous *"Fire and Ice"* poem:

Some say the world will end in fire,
Some say in ice.
From what I've tasted of desire
I hold with those who favor fire.
But if it had to perish twice,
I think I know enough of hate
To say that for destruction ice
Is also great
And would suffice

The flower of life image is a modern, new age adopted symbol dating back to around 500 BCE in Egypt, carved into walls. This is also a Dutch symbol called the *Glückstern*, or luck-star, whose meaning is linked to that of Hagalaz and the web of Wyrd and was used as a talisman for magickal workings. The seed or flower of life is also created of 60° isometrics, but with overlapping circles instead of triangles. When the runes were created, we were still carving bones and wood with knives, and thus the need for straight line symbology was important, particularly as a widely used alphabet. When you look at the flower of life, it represents the initial cell division of a gamete as seen through a microscope. It is the undifferentiated stage of life, be it plant, fungi or animal, where there is not yet any consolidation into form. If we round off the web of Wyrd a little you can also see the physical form of cell division, i.e. the beginning of life.

A question one should ask is how a six-pointed symbol could come to represent the ninth rune? Nine is the most holy of numbers in Nordic culture, where it represents the number of days and nights Odin hung on his spear, the number of worlds on Yggdrasil, the tree of life, and is repeated many times in Norse mythos, such as Heimdall's nine mothers and Thor's nine final steps. So, nine is important cosmologically, but why the six points in Hagalaz? Here I will refer to a Nicholas Tesla quote: "If you only knew the magnificence of the 3, 6 and 9, then you would have a key to the universe." No one quite understands this quote, as I don't believe anyone quite understands Hagalaz fully, but theories explain that it relates to the bisection of a circle into equal parts and how they will all sum to 9 (e.g. 360° = 3+6+0 = 9, or 45° = 4 + 5 = 9, etc.) There is a pattern where circular division is important for 9, but 6 is also important, as 60° is another equal partition to a circle (60° = 6 + 0 = 6). Therefore, 6 is also part of the 3, 6, 9 universal concept. One could say that 6 and 9 are two aspects of the same three-dimensional concept of which the Egyptians, the Norse and Tesla all had some level of understanding.

10. Nauthiz

[now-theez]: the phonetic 'n' sound, as in need, nerve, or net.

Nauthiz! Need. Necessity. The need-fire. Nauthiz is about the things you need, whether they are basic human needs or emotional needs. There is a feeling of constriction, or lacking, that comes with that need, and the energy of Nauthiz is not one of reassurance or comfort.

Nauthiz represents a need or a desire, one that burns and must be filled. It drives us, pushes us to our limits to think outside our boxes and do whatever we can to obtain what we need. It is the driver of innovation and technology. Where in Kenaz we had our tools, our knowledge and made things out of passion, Nauthiz is when we need make our tools, build our knowledge over again and create for survival. Do not baulk if you do not at first succeed. Creating something out of nothing is hard and you won't build a palace out of sticks alone, but you can make shelter to ensure that you are safe and well enough to get up the next day and keep going.

Nauthiz can be picking up the pieces after a catastrophic Hagalaz type of event. Where Hagalaz is ice and fire, Nauthiz is fire and Isa is ice. But the destruction of Hagalaz is past, and Nauthiz better represents the inner discomfort in the aftermath. After a traumatic event one should first ask themselves, "Okay, what do I need?". It is in this that we learn what is actually important, be it food, water, shelter, clothing, fire or just emotional support.

This is the second of the three Norns, representing Verdandi, or the present. Verdandi is known as "that which is coming into being" and is a point where we make a choice. We are asked to focus on the now, forgetting past and future, to gather what we need in this instant. We are asked to take care of the self, such as putting on our breathing mask in a metaphorical plane that is crashing.

One of the most important messages in Nauthiz is that it might represent a need, but it is also simultaneously the fulfillment of that need. Our needs are met. We are safe. We may be uncomfortable and needing to be innovative, but we can build that fire; we can feed that desire. With enough inner work, and paying attention to where our traumas lie, we can sort out what each of our needs are bit-by-bit, and find we have the power to meet all of them.

The image of Nauthiz is that of a bow drill made of a vertical stick spun quickly using a crosswise bow. It uses friction to create heat and smouldering embers as a fire starter. It is a perfect representation of innovation, driven by the very basic need for heat and food. Man is back in his most basic element, using whatever tools are at his disposal. The base of the bow drill shows multiple holes, which is normal, but represents how this is a lesson that will be repeated. It can take many attempts before one is successful. The grey is the smoke, which represents uncertainty and conveys discomfort. Grey is also a medium between black, like the void found in Hagalaz, and the pure white snow of Isa. Somehow, I have always seen this rune as green. Perhaps because of the relation of desire and envy, but I think also because it takes that heart-focus to bring success in this situation.

There is a particularly deep, dark pit that represents merkstave Nauthiz when our desires become overwhelming. This can come in the form of forcing those desires onto other people (e.g. assault), or in addictions, where we feel trapped in cycles, feeling nothing but constrictions when we don't have our vices. But that discomfort exists for a reason. It is a symptom of need to be faced honestly. We need to meet those challenges and grow as a person, finding ways to make ourselves feel okay without causing harm to ourselves or others. Use of this rune in the correct configuration can help people overcome these destructive patterns.

If you find yourself with a merkstave Nauthiz, the need has turned into a problematic issue, either for yourself or in others. You may be denying yourself an unmet need or have fallen into addiction patterns. Take the time to be mindful and aware, and take space away from others if you need, until you can sort through your issues.

It is because of the dark side that I associate this rune particularly with the mischievous god Loki. Loki is a force of chaos and destruction that one can argue is equated with Hagalaz, but I think, overall, he suits Nauthiz better. He will happily, madly, push folks to their limits, but at the end of those experiences everyone ends up in improved situations. For example, the story where Loki slandered all the gods at dinner and later turned into a salmon, he upset everyone and was punished. But in doing so, he also created the fishing net that was needed to catch him, which was an invaluable tool for humanity. It can be like following the devil, if one wants to make that comparison, where the fall into temptation and desire may not have been a pleasant experience, but one walks away with a better sense of self.

11. Isa

[ee-sah]: the phonetic 'ee' sound, as in sleep, dream, or keep.[4]

Isa - Ice. It is a representation of stillness and turning inward. It is when we set our emotions and problems aside for when we are grounded and better able to deal with them. Isa tells us to just stop, let things be as they are and focus on keeping our energy still. This is the time to pause and reflect, not act.

Isa is a rune that is somewhat simple to explain but, as always, there is a greater depth of understanding the more time one spends working with any rune. It is essentially a hermitage, a closing off from the world to seek inner peace and wisdom. It is greatly linked with meditation and provides a way to focus or still the ego so one can take in more of what is surrounding them.

I find this rune comes often in emotionally turbulent times. It is not always a warning, but usually just good advice. Taking a moment to find inner peace can be useful in both ups and downs. For example, I've found this rune to sometimes mean that I need to not be too excited about something because there might come disappointment later, or the reverse, where I need to not be upset because if I just wait a bit there will be good things after.

I find the 'i' shape of the rune to be very useful in understanding its vibration. It is sort of like a zipper, a closing off or sealing of something. I often draw a line over my body, from chin down, to act out that zipping or closing action when using this rune.

The image of Isa is that of an icicle. It represents the cold, still iciness of winter, when everything is frozen and calm. It is peaceful and beautiful, rather than rash and hard, but there is still a coldness about it. It can be seen as positive or negative, but the truth is that it is neither, it just is. The ice also links back to the icy realm of Niflheim and is thus part of the primordial flow from which all life is created.

---

4. It is also related to the short 'i' sound in English, and I see Isa in the words ice, inwards, and I.

Isa is the last of the three Norn runes and represents Skuld, or the future. Skuld is known as "debt" or consequences, coming after the choice we make in Nauthiz. The future is often chaotic and messy and will be full of ups and downs. When one is looking ahead to their fate, they must be open and still. Most of all, they must be able to set aside their ego and see the bigger picture. One must also think of the future to be able to set aside things and find stillness in the moment; they must know that the spring will once again melt the snow and the time for activity will come again. This is similar to how jays stash food for winter, or how bears go into hibernation in preparation for the spring.

In the wake of Hagalaz, Isa is what finally brings us to a place where we can process what has happened. Hagalaz represented both ice and fire, and was the crisis. Nauthiz was the fire and now Isa is the ice aspect. Nauthiz was the immediate "need" response where we did the work to be safe and now, in Isa, we can reflect and learn in the aftermath. Isa asks us to take our time, be slow, be mindful, and process that which has happened so we can move forward into the future when spring has come again.

Isa has no merkstave, representing that stillness is neither good nor bad, it simply is. One could argue that the opposite of a freeze is a thaw, or the opposite of stillness is motion. But motion and warmth are aspects of other runes, such as Raidho, which can be applied to Isa to soften it. The lack of an inverse of Isa, however, makes its meaning very clear and without ambiguity.

12. Jera

[yehr-ah]: the phonetic 'y' sound, as in year, yellow or yard.[5]

Jera. This rune means "year," and the German word for year is Jahr. Jera relates to the annual rotation of the earth and the harvest that comes with fall. This rune says that in order to reap the reward of a successful harvest one must first sow ample seeds and put in the work tending them throughout the year. If you do, you will be more likely to find good fortune, otherwise you may find yourself lacking.

Jera is a rune of change, an inevitable force of nature. Its primary symbol is that of harvest, but the harvest is a year-long process. This rune falls after the midwinter of Isa when we are planning our planting for the spring. However, the harvest and wheat aspect of this rune relate also to late summer and autumn. Winter is also an aspect of Jera, as harvests are what keep us alive throughout cold winters. So, Jera simultaneously represents the entire year, all the seasons and all the transitions between them.

So how does one reap a successful harvest? It is about hard work and brings forth the adage "You shall reap what you sow." There is so much more than just dropping some seeds in the ground and seeing what happens! There is plowing the soil, planting the seeds, tending the crops, watering the fields and managing the pests. The actual harvest involves work with a scythe, storing the grains and keeping your bounty from spoiling. Then you must finally mill your grains and bake your bread before you can actually enjoy the fruits of your labour. Each step is done with knowledge of what comes next, in a timely and practiced manner, and with some level of good fortune. Even if you luck out with no pests and perfect weather, without the efforts done properly in preparation you will still end up with little, or nothing!

If you find you have failed at any one step along the way and are disheartened, remember there is always next year. The harvest will come again, as will your chance to

---

5. In Germanic languages the 'j' is pronounced like a 'y.'

sow, and then you will be armed with better knowledge. Each year is different, and with each year we grow and learn. This is the nature of time, which only flows forward. Jera says to not give up, try again next time. This applies not just when it comes to farming, but in any endeavour. Jera is a nature-based lesson but is relevant to employment and earning also, where the synchronization of hard work and luck will bring about wealth.

In the cycle of the runes Jera comes directly after the three Norns. The space between it and the next rune, Eihwaz, is the midpoint of the cycle. It is asking us, the hero, how well we did in that traumatic endeavour. How hard did we work to meet our needs, if we did so mindfully, and if we took the space that we needed to isolate when we were asked to. Did we put in the hard work necessary to reap rewards? Jera is a respite, where even if we did not deal with the ordeal very well, we can be assured the worst is over; it has passed and we can enjoy our place of solace even if we aren't surrounded by the abundance we wanted.

Jera is related to the goddess Jörd, the jotun (giantess) mother of Thor. Jörd is pronounced like "yard," and this goddess of golden hair is linked to grass and wheat. It is because of her that we call our patch of greenery outside our homes our yards. Jörd is a fertility goddess of the earth who connects with Odin, the father of the sky, to birth the heroic figure of Thor, who defends Asgard. This is the timeless tale of mother earth and father sky pairing together in harmony to create a new and wonderful heroic god.

Drawn around the rune I have included a representation of a medicine wheel, a Native American spiritual symbol that represents the seasons as they rotate around the circle. The four-pointed wheel is also found in Europe as the sun cross. This symbol is also the astrological symbol for the Earth. These are a great example of the universality of symbols; multiple cultures drew the same symbol linked to the same cosmic vibration.

The image of Jera is unique in the runes, in that it is composed of two sections that are unattached. The two halves are an image of rotation, as each is in balance and harmony as they perpetually twist and orbit one another. There is no merkstave position for this rune, no negative or repressed version, it simply is what it is and there is no right or wrong about it.

13. Eihwaz

[eye-wahz]: the phonetics of this rune are uncertain, and is generally presumed to be somewhere between an 'i' and an 'e,' transcribed as æ.[6]

Eihwaz. The yew tree. This rune signifies travel between the worlds of Yggdrasil, including that to the realm of the dead. These are the worlds which lie beneath this one, those which only our subconscious mind can sense. Eihwaz is a release of the self, a removal of the senses that we associate with life. The deepest level of this journey is not for the faint of heart, but this realm is one which we touch regularly—in our dreams, with our intuition and during meditation.

The yew tree was planted in ancient graveyards as it was said to be connected to the world of the dead. There are several reasons for this, one being that the yew was said to be able to resurrect itself from its branches. Yews also grow slowly, for what seems like an eternity to humans, with lifespans of up to 5,000 years. They hold this history in their annual tree rings and are ancient wisdom keepers. Most prominently, the yew bark is toxic and contains a mixture of potent chemicals that are, to this day, used as medicine to treat parasites, breast cancer, kidney and liver issues, and can trigger miscarriages as abortifacients. The seeds within the berries are also highly toxic and can kill livestock as well as humans. I have also read that the chemicals emitted by yew trees can induce a psychedelic state in people who are sitting or sleeping under them. They may then believe they are speaking with the dead, not understanding why they entered a heightened state of awareness. This myriad of characteristics makes the yew a sacred and ancient plant with much wisdom and is understandably highly associated with death.

Yggdrasil is the world tree that spans the universe, holding the nine worlds. It reaches from the lower realms with its roots to the most upper realms with its branches. The roots are where the lower worlds dwell, that of Helheim (the world of

---

[6]. In general, this rune is used less in writing and more commonly in magickal workings.

the dead), Muspelheim (the realm of fire) and Niflheim (the realm of ice), and where the great dragon Nidhogg gnaws upon Yggdrasil's roots. The upper realms of Asgard (home of the Aesir gods), Alfheim (home of the elves) and Vanaheim (home of the Vanir gods) are held above in its branches, where a great eagle sits. Midgard, more commonly known as Earth, is where we are located and is present in the center of the tree, with Jotunheim (home of the giants) and Svartalfheim (home of the dwarves or dark elves) somewhere around it. There is a squirrel, Rattatoskr, who likes to insult everyone as he travels up and down the trunk of the tree sending messages from the gods to the beings of the other worlds.

Yggdrasil is sometimes said to be an ash tree, likely because of the doming shape of the canopy that looks like it could hold an entire world. Ash is also said to be the wood from which the first man, Ask, was created, while the source of the first woman, Embla, is less clear but could be elm or vine. Personally, I associate her with alder, which is similar to birch and is a meaning contained in the rune Berkano.

The image of Eihwaz represents the trunk of the world tree, though Eihwaz is yew and not ash. Travelling up and down Yggdrasil's trunk is the transference of a spirit or consciousness between one realm and another. There is a sense of movement and travel as one leaves this world and senses behind to journey forth and experience consciousness in another way. This is not a physical journey, but a spiritual one.

Eihwaz is a rune of many mystical properties and can be used in any kind of shamanic or magickal working, whenever one needs to access energies beyond the physical realm. For example, it can be used to speak with our ancestors and unearth ancient knowledge. It can also be used to deepen one's state of meditation or induce frequent and powerful dreaming. Eihwaz can even be used in ceremonial magick, activating of the kundalini serpent in eastern practices and connecting with one's spirit guides. It can also help one find their way back from these realms.

I very often find this rune comes up when people are using psychoactive substances, as entheogens are another mode of altering one's consciousness. Eihwaz can thus be used as a protective tool when one is embarking on such journeys, not to ground, but to help one find their way and direct them to what they need to know.

There is also a sense of relief and movement in Eihwaz, of letting go and shedding all the weight of experiencing this life. Letting go of the senses is one interpretation, but it can also be a metaphorical death in the sense that we are leaving behind something that may no longer be serving us. Where Raidho represented a journey forth, from which we usually return, Eihwaz is more final, where there is no going back after experiencing a death. This could signal the end of a job, relationship, or any other experience which we are done with and are now ready to move on to the next stage. Think of a caterpillar and how it has to undergo a type of death of the self to transform into a beautiful butterfly that can flutter free of the plant to which it has been stuck. We may not be able to turn back in death, but there is a sense of freedom and release that comes with it. Thankfully, most Eihwaz journeys are ones we do return from, as we can usually move both up and down the trunk, but we always come back a little bit different when we encounter the other worlds.

This death is where Eihwaz comes into the sequence of the runes. It follows the harvest as we move on after reaping rewards. This is the little death of our hero, where he finally leaves the rubble of Hagalaz behind. He knows that there is nothing here for him any longer, and it is time to move on and become a stronger and better version of himself. This is an important part of healing from trauma, when we let go of it and are free to move on to become a newer, improved person.

The last imagery I put into this painting is the shadowed creatures. These creatures, such as fairies, trolls and dragons, do not exist on physical Earth as we know it. We can only interact with them by extending our consciousness outside of this reality and finding them in their native worlds that lie parallel to ours.

There is no merkstave position of Eihwaz. Death can be seen as negative or positive, but both aspects come at the same time together, and death itself is a neutral force.

14. Perthro

[per-throw]: the phonetic 'p' sound, as in play, pawn, pendulum or pink.

Perthro. The word translates to 'dice cup' or 'chess piece.' This rune speaks to the mysteries of luck and fate of an individual. Perthro is a great win for some, but for others it is an unending burden. Not everyone is born equally and we all encounter moments where we are subject to this higher force that determines events in our lives.

Some of you might not believe in luck or fate, but if so, I would say it is likely you are one who hasn't experienced the extremes that fate can be. Everyone has their up and down moments. Sometimes it is related to the choice of an individual, but not always. Not everyone has an equal chance from the start. Think of how some people are born with birth defects. They are not given an equal footing from the start as everyone else; they lack the same opportunities. But from great misfortune sometimes the most fortunate circumstances come, and many people power through and find meaning from it.

The Norse believed in not just one but two aspects of fate, called Wyrd, which we have encountered in Hagalaz, and Orlog. Wyrd is our destiny, something like how we play the hand of cards we have been dealt. Wyrd is the circumstances that we have control over, the aspect of luck and fate that our actions and choices change. Wyrd has been laid out for us by the Norns, but with the expectation that we will weave this part of the pattern ourselves. We have to work to grasp it or we will find misfortune. Orlog is described as the fate that we lack control over, the threads which have been woven in a more permanent manner by the Norns upon our coming into this world. To tune into your Orlog, you must accept yourself in both strengths and weaknesses and see that they are what make you perfect for your destiny. You are equipped with what you need to achieve your purpose in this life. Realization of your Orlog will help you to go with the flow and accept the things you cannot change.

Tuning into synchronicities is a good way of paying attention to what the Fates have in store for you. Examples of Perthro can be the times when you encounter the person you were thinking of in a coffee shop, find that exact thing you needed in that exact moment, you randomly see the clock at 11:11 or see an animal cross your path that has spiritual meaning related to your predicament. These are messages from the higher powers and patterns of things telling you that you are on the right track. You're in the exact right moment that you are supposed to be at this time, you are seeing the threads of Wyrd.

The most obvious image of Perthro is that of a dice-throwing cup. The dice game represented here is the game Spears and Shields, a recent game inspired by Nordic dice games. The chess board is of the game Hnefatafl, where the object is for the white pieces to escort their king off the board, and the black pawns to try to stop them from doing so. The chess piece is another image that Perthro is said to represent. The dice are pure luck, whereas Hnefatafl is pure strategy. Both dice and chess games were played in the Viking era. Games were not just a fun past time as the luck and ability that went with the games helped the Norse decide who made good warriors and strategists. The luck that one had in games was said to be tied to the luck one had on the battlefield and in life.

The other image Perthro is said to represent is the womb. The cup is also a metaphor for the womb, in which luck and fate play out when the egg is fertilized by the sperm. It is also in this womb when the Norns spin their threads of fate. Water is highly linked here because of the well from which the Norns draw souls.

In the sequence of the runes the womb comes immediately after the rune of death because, in this point of the journey, the hero is experiencing a rebirth. The actual birth happens in rune eighteen, with the next three runes being something like the three trimesters of pregnancy. Perthro signals the beginning of this new stage of the journey, after the death and release that happened previously in Eihwaz. The die has been cast, the cards laid out on the table, and now we wait to see what happens next.

Sometimes we will find that no matter how hard we try we simply cannot seem to move forward. It can feel like running on a treadmill and never getting anywhere. This is the merkstave meaning of Perthro, when we are in the wrong place and life won't let us continue on this same path. It can take some time to discern between those places that we are not meant to be and when life has just put a more difficult obstacle in our way to make our resolve even stronger. Merkstave Perthro does not necessarily mean that now is the time to give up, it can also mean that you just can't see the higher purpose to whatever it is that you are struggling with at the moment. Turning misfortune into fortune is the pinnacle of good luck.

15. Algiz

[al-geez]: the phonetic 'z' sound, as in buzz or dazzle.[7]

ALGIZ. The elk. The swan. A splayed hand. The Valkyries. The sacred grove. The sedge. The Bifröst. There are many symbols entwined in Algiz, but they ultimately mean the same thing: divine protection. This rune represents a sacred space where one cannot be harmed. The gods are watching from above and this is your space to find connection to them. Algiz is again a representation of Yggdrasil, namely the outstretched roots and branches. Where Eihwaz represented travel and movement through the trunk of Yggdrasil, Algiz is now the destination. Here we find pause in what we were seeking, though maybe we didn't know that this is what we had been looking for. Perthro was a cast of the dice, a synchronous sign in the right direction that happened to lead us where we need to be. We found ourselves within the womb and it is here in Algiz that we open our eyes in the safety and comfort of that womb. We can spend time here with that knowledge.

The stretching of the branches shows a direct connection to the gods. They have created this sacred space, a grove where Yggdrasil grows that you have to find. They watch over you, and by reaching out to them you can receive their blessings. There is a rainbow bridge, the Bifröst, that connects their realm of Asgard to ours, and it is through signs such as these that you can find their presence. This is the closest rune to Heimdall, as he guards this bridge holding the Gjallarhorn in his hands, the horn which will signal Ragnarok.

The Valkyries are women that deliver the spirits of the dead from the battlefield to Odin's hall, Valhalla. They have been said to have wings, and their animal totem is that of the swan with white wings. Algiz is sometimes said to represent a swan in flight

---

[7]. 'Z' is much more common in German, in words such as zwischen (between), zurück (return) and Zauber (magick).

and is thus linked to the Valkyries. This rune is used for protection in battle and for connection with the Valkyries so they may find you if you fall.

The most common representation the image of Algiz is said to represent is that of an elk's antlers. The elk is a majestic creature, with long reaching antlers similar to branches, another representation of a connection to the gods. The times I have seen elk in the wilderness they have stood tall and proud and were quite the sight to behold, with a mane akin to that of a lion. I have also encountered elk multiple times within the spirit realm and can speak to their powerful, otherworldly connection. Moose are known as elk in Scandinavia, where what I know as elk are called wapiti. Red deer, closely related to wapiti/elk, are called 'king deer' in Flemish, reflecting how the Germanic peoples were in awe of these wonderful creatures. The extinct Irish elk had even more impressive antlers than any of these existing species. It can be said that, although Algiz means 'elk' and may have originally been intended for moose, any great antlered creature of the forest is represented by Algiz.

The shape is also said to be that of a splayed hand, or of a person reaching their arms to the gods in praise. This is again in relation to protection through divine connection.

Algiz merkstave is a sign that you need protection. You need to find your sacred space, which I often find can be easiest when connecting with animals. It does not mean that you won't be protected, but it suggests you should pay attention to what you need to distance yourself from at this time. This inverse position is also a focus on the roots, rather than the branches of Yggdrasil. There is a version of Algiz that has no merkstave, where there are not three lines that reach upward but two downward, signifying roots, but in the most common set of the Futhark we tend to look at the branches and roots separately.

The lower realm, the world of the roots, is seen as dark and unpleasant by many. This is where Helheim is, where the souls that did not die honourably were sent. The part known as Nastrond is where the dragon Nidhogg, known as "He Who Strikes with Malice" chews on the roots of Yggdrasil and devours the souls of the perjurers, murderers and adulterers. In shamanism, the lower realm is largely understood to be the source of creation. This is the source of knowledge and where the souls of the animals exist, and where we can go to find our own well of power and insight within ourselves. Going downward in the tree of life, though not as glamorous as a journey upward, is sometimes just as important when we need answers, or to find safety and protection.

16. Sowilo

[soh-wee-low]: the phonetic 's' sound, as in son, shine, strength, and success.

Sowilo is the Sun, the goddess Sol. The sun is a universal symbol for success, triumph and light. Its shining rays are what bring life to the earth, motivation into our days and joy into our hearts. The glow of Sowilo will be what drives you to victory over your circumstances. Sowilo often appears on bright sunny days and with the joyful feelings that come with them.

Sowilo is the reward at the end of Heimdall's aett for the long and difficult journey we have made. It began at Hagalaz when our community and safety was pulled out from underneath of us. We have now found security and joy within ourselves as individuals. This separates it from the joy in the collective community of Wunjo, which was the reward at the end of Freya's aett.

Sowilo is the part of the journey where the hero has experienced death in Eihwaz and is in the midst of his rebirth. After connecting with the gods and ourselves in the previous rune of Algiz we now find we have the tools within ourselves to go forth into the world and conquer the giants. The hero sees himself in his full light. It is the second trimester of pregnancy, where the mother is glowing and joyful and everyone is happy for the new family's success.

This rune I see as being connected to Baldur, the son of Odin who was said to be the shining one. Everyone loved Baldur— every plant, god and animal. He was kind and charming and intelligent, and he brought joy to Asgard. For those who have studied Kabbalah, Baldur is one of the few Norse gods I say fits well into a Sephira, being of the sun and therefore of Tephirath.

But the sun itself was the goddess Sol, a feminine energy. In Raidho we were introduced to her, as she is the rune of the sun's path. Sowilo is the rune of the sun

itself, and its radiant energy. The goddess Sol was made of fire, a spark of Muspelheim during the creation of the world. Norse paganism is one of the few spiritual paths in which the sun is represented as female and the moon as being male. This reflects the importance of women and their power in Nordic tradition, for at the time women had more control over money and the household than other European cultures. Norse women also went to battle alongside men, and analysis of the bones left behind after battle has shown that almost as many women as men wielded spears and swords. These shield-maidens were as fierce and strong as their male counterparts, whom represented by the moon, born of the ice of Niflheim, were more regarded as being calm and supportive.

There is a common bindrune of Sowilo that consists of two of this rune, offset together to make not one ray but the solar wheel. This is known as the Swastika, and is a very powerful rune for victory, not just in war but on an individual level. The symbol was seen in many early European and Asian cultures and was widely and commonly used for many reasons. It is highly unfortunate that this rune was used by the German Nazi party during their time of power. This should be used as a warning, for those who try to fly to close to the sun will be burned. This rune is powerful, but you must use it in moderation and for the right reasons.

There is no merkstave version of Sowilo. The singular ray itself has no way it can go wrong. Success, power, victory, inner light and a place of power are all there. Enjoy your day, enjoy life and have no worries in this moment.

Tyr's Aett

TYR IS A MYSTERIOUS FIGURE IN NORSE MYTHOS. He plays an important role in the sacrifice of his hand to bind the wolf Fenrir to delay the coming of Ragnarok (see Tiwaz description). Sometimes he is said to be Odin's adopted son of the giants Hymir and Hrodr. Other times he is placed as Aesir family, as the son of Odin and the daughter of Hymir. Regardless, Tyr, like many of Odin's sons, has jotun heritage.

Tyr's hall is not mentioned in the poem *Grímnismál*. It seems odd to me that the god of law and order, and the patron of the Althing (an assembly of lawspeakers), that Tyr would not have a hall. Whether Tyr's hall was just a piece of information that was lost, or if he truly did not have one is up to speculation and lost to history.

Tyr is perhaps evolved from the Indo-European god Dyeus worshipped around 5,000 years ago. Dyeus was a central god, the Sky Father, who can also be compared to the Greek god Zeus. Dyeus was the god to whom oaths were sworn. In the Viking age Tyr's role became less central than Dyeus, but he was still known as the god of justice, law and war, and oaths were sworn to him. Tyr was an honourable warrior who taught strength and sacrifice for the greater good, but would first promote pacts, legal agreements and truces.

The Romans viewed Tyr as similar to Mars, their god of war. Tyr is thus attributed to Tuesday (Tyr's day), the day of Mars. However, Tyr's history as the central sky god places him better into the role of Jupiter, attributed to Thor and Thursday. This ambiguity is one of the reasons I don't believe the Norse pantheon fits well into the Kabbalah system used by many magick practitioners.

This image portrays Tyr's strength and kindness. Tyr here has lines of wisdom at the corners of his eyes that reflect his experiences. The Tyr I drew is meant to appear as a warrior to not be crossed, but also as a caring listener to whom you can turn to for sound judgement. The howling wolf Fenrir haunts him in the background.

The first aett was a material journey (the physical change from a singular unit to that of a larger synergistic community), the second aett was personal development (isolation and hard lessons that led us to enlightenment), and this third aett is honour. The story of Tyr's aett begins with a return to humanity. Sacrificing our safety is the first lesson. We then birth back into the world, find how to work with others, heal, become grounded and then end with the blessing of honour in family. This is a circular ending that begins again at Freya's aett. The journey through the first two aetts was necessary for our hero to find this higher calling in this final aett, after which he can rest before beginning a new journey.

17. Tiwaz

[tee-wahz]: the phonetic 't' sound, as in Tyr, titan, truth and trust.

Tiwaz is the rune of Tyr, the god of justice. It is the first of the final aett of runes, the aett of Tyr. This rune is representative of balance, laws and compromise. It represents that which provides structure and order in appeasement to both sides of an issue. You will win your battle through truth, sacrifice and thoughtfulness.

Tyr is the god of war, and the image of Tiwaz is said to be that of a spear point. War was believed to measure justice, where the victor was the one who had been blessed by the gods that day. Tyr's not a violent fighter, however. This title is given to Thor (Thurisaz) who slays giants on a daily basis. Tyr's role was that of the peacemaker, ruling over treaties, assemblies and balance, rather than brute force.

This shows that Tyr, though having an aspect of fiery Mars, is more closely attributed to air. Air is the element attributed to mental acuity and, when the Tiwaz rune comes forth, the message is that your victory must be achieved through intellect, not force. This is also a very true aspect of war and chess, as often your opponent's strength in numbers can be overrun by greater strategy.

The most infamous act of Tyr was the sacrifice of his hand to the great wolf Fenrir in an attempt to delay Ragnarok and save the world. Fenrir was one of the spawns of the mischief god Loki and the jotun Angerboda; the others being Hel, she who ruled the dead, and Jörmungandr, the serpent that encircled the world. These offspring were fated to bring about the end of gods and man, and so the Aesir needed to mercifully deal with them. They had decided to chain Fenrir in a magickal rope forged by the dwarves—from things that no longer exist because they were used to make the rope, such as the sound of a cat's paws and the roots of mountains. To trick Fenrir into allowing the gods to fetter him, they told the wolf they wanted to test his strength

and that they would remove the rope afterwards. Tyr placed his right hand in the mouth of the great wolf to show the wolf that they did not mean harm. Once Fenrir was caught, he realized he could not get free and he bit Tyr's hand off. Fenrir will be freed during Ragnarok, but it is another great hound, Garm, the hound of Hel, who is destined to kill Tyr at the end of days.

One of the most important messages of the Tiwaz rune is embedded in this story. The Aesir gods were committing to an act that was unjust. Loki was one of the Aesir, and they betrayed him by imprisoning one of his children, tricking Fenrir into submission. The gods themselves were committing crimes and acting outside the law in what they believed to be a greater purpose in delaying Ragnarok. Nothing was more important to them than this at the time, and even their honour and laws were set aside for this purpose. So, one message of Tiwaz is that sometimes we must do unthinkable acts in the name of a higher purpose. But then we also must pay for them, and in this story the sacrifice was that of Tyr's hand. Tyr was the only god brave enough to stick his hand in the mouth of the wolf, and the hero of the tale for taking the entire punishment for the dishonourable deed they had done.

I also would like to point out the duality of wolves in Germanic beliefs. Fenrir is a dreadful figure in Norse mythos, and Garm is no more appealing a character. Wolves would kill cattle and were likely one of the major adversaries of Nordic ways of life. But there are two benevolent wolves that sit at Odin's feet, named Geri and Freki. Geri and Freki translate to 'ravenous' and 'greedy,' and were said to feast on the dead after battles on Midgard. Though this sounds macabre, it is a realistic reflection of how wolves have large appetites and is also an important reflection of their link to carrion feeding ravens like Hugin and Munin. Geri and Freki were said to also have accompanied the humans after they were created by Odin, where wolves' understanding of companionship and tribe were the knowledge that they passed onto humans so we could learn to form societies. There are also Norse tales in the Volsung Saga of a hero who was raised by two wolves, highlighting again their value and importance as being more than just monstrous creatures of the night.

The figure seated on the throne in the image is that of Tyr, his gaze forward and piercing in judgement. He holds Odin's mythical spear, the Gungnir, which never misses its target in his hand. This accentuates the spearhead shape of the Tiwaz rune.

The shadow of a wolf, be it Garm or Fenrir, stalks him in the background, which is also reminiscent of Odin and one of his wolves that sit at his feet. The wolves are representations of day and night, darkness and light, and this rune is the balance or decision between one and the other. The spear-point shape is said to be that of a pillar, or Irminsul, that holds the heavens above earth, which is how I have used the rune here.

In the sequence of the runes, Tiwaz correlates with the third trimester of pregnancy. The expecting mother is on the last stretch before the birth. She is tired, sore, and feeling ready to get this part over with to meet her soon-to-be child, sacrificing her own comfort for the wellbeing of her little one. It can be a long, tough and enduring trial when the glowing light of Sowilo is no longer filling our awareness and we find ourselves dealing with the more difficult parts of reality. This last trimester feels like it goes on forever and the birth can't come quickly enough. This is when the hero prepares to leave the safety of his sanctuary of Algiz, carrying with him the glow of Sowilo. He is now looking forward, ready to face the next trials that life will bring his way. He is making the just decision to go back into the world.

Merkstave Tiwaz represents a trial that does not go favourably. This could mean you have been judged as the one who is unworthy, or guilty of a crime. It is time to reflect and see where you may have gone wrong, and what actions you might have done that were unjust. Or perhaps it is simply one of life's many challenges that is not going fairly or justly, but you must keep your eye on the bigger picture and realize that these challenges have a greater purpose and meaning to them. Now is the time to take the judgement that has been given with honour and humility.

18. Berkano

[bear-kan-oh]: the phonetic 'b' sound, as in baby, birth, breast, beauty and birch.

BERKANO. Berkana. Beorc. The birch. Berkano's literal meaning is "birch tree," which is known as the mother of the forest. This rune relates strongly to the earthy feminine energy, the mother, the breast, the baby, the birth and all other aspects of nature that are related to the woman. Berkano speaks of the birthing phase of magick, when the seed that has been germinating has come to full term and is now freed into the wider world.

The birch tree is the mother of a developing forest. After a forest fire, or other interruption, the birch will often grow first. The birch grows fast and dies fast, leaving their rotting nurse logs to create a new forest after they have gone. Thus, the birch tree is a symbol of motherhood and birth. It is a nurturing energy that is equated with femininity.

This is the final step of the death/rebirth cycle in our hero's journey after he has passed Tyr's judgement. The three trimester runes have passed, which were largely a time of peace and introspection. Our hero has learned of his connection to the divine, his light and his truth, and is armed and truly ready to go out into the world again. He is stronger than he once was. He learned the lessons of Hagal and the three Norns, and though he may be coming from a place of safety, like a baby, he is a new and better person.

Berkano is a rune of gentleness and feminine energy, the divine feminine if you will, where Tyr was strongly masculine. All humans are a balance of both, and this rune is the feminine to balance the masculine, Venus to balance Mars, Yin to balance the Yang. Our hero is now in touch with his feminine side as well as masculine, and truly ready for his birth back into the world. Let us recall that Sol is feminine and that

the sun, rather than the moon, represents femininity to the old Germanic peoples. The fires of Sol are that of power and expression, the female warrior. Now, Berkano is the grounded and earthy feminine, the mother, the nurturer, a soft and receptive tenderness. But in Ingwaz we will see that there is powerful earth energy in the masculine, as all four elements of fire, air, water and earth have both masculine and feminine expressions.

Berkano is related to physical, mental and spiritual aspects of women. It is in the way women look, walk, grow their hair, their voice, their curves and their soft skin. It is in their tenderness, their receptivity, their ability to take on many tasks, to care and nurture and to love unconditionally. This rune is very similar to the Empress card of the tarot.

Another symbol within Berkano is that of the bear. The word 'bear' (Bär in German) is in the root of Berkano and is thus in the word itself. The bear is powerful mother energy. She is the keeper of the forest who protectively tends her young for several years. She is peaceful but fierce when needed. Bear spirit is also highly linked with plant medicine, as she not only understands their medicine but is also a catalyst in spreading seeds through her scat to help create and birth new plants.

The image of Berkano is that of breasts, where each of the points are nipples. The breast is that from which the baby feeds and is again a symbol of femininity. In my painting I chose not to directly paint this image to keep my work free to share on any media, but instead created the image of a mother with a babe at her breast, which hints at the shape and image.

Berkano merkstave is a disconnection from the feminine. This may represent an imbalance of masculine energy, or dishonouring your feminine self, such as using sexuality in a way that is unhealthy. Or perhaps your birth, that thing which you attempted to bring forth into the world, has failed.

19. Ehwaz

[eh-wahz]: the phonetic short 'e' sound, as in eleven, telepathy, and empathy.

EHWAZ IS THE HORSE, OR MORE ACCURATELY, THE RELATIONSHIP OF THE HORSE AND RIDER. This is the rune of co-operation, of balanced understanding in an unbreakable bond. It is about harmony and the balancing of opposites, the joining of two to become one mind. This is about love that transcends all verbal communication, where the horse and rider both play equal but different roles. This rune may be used to find common ground, strengthen a friendship, find love, synergize other runes or develop a mutually beneficial business relationship with a boss or co-worker.

The relationship of the horse and the rider is primarily one of business where the human is the brain and the horse is the brawn, but there is an understanding between the two that they both need and care for each other. There is no lust in this relationship, but there is a strong bond of love and respect. The horse refers to Sleipnir, Odin's eight-legged steed who was faster than any other horse. He was born of Loki, who is a male but transformed himself into a mare when he conceived Sleipnir. This also suggests a balance of the feminine and masculine. Sleipnir is related to shamanism, as Odin's mount has travelled the nine worlds with him on his back. The message here is that together, two people (including non-human persons such as horses), are able to travel to new places and achieve greater things than if they were alone.

When I say a business type of relationship, what probably brings to mind is a rather dry and unromantic visual of two people in an office, so let me clarify that business is just as important an aspect of marriage as lust. In marriage two people must co-ordinate structure within a home over finances, children, food, material property, expectations, tasks and time for each other. There is a constant push and pull from

both parties over roles, how much work each person takes on and whether or not staying together is beneficial in the future. Boundaries are important.

Even with all the work, love is still a beautiful thing! That two people can come together and be able to communicate and work all of those aspects needed for a successful partnership is nothing short of a miracle. True love is a combination of care, surrender and trust; when we give another being the reins we trust in their instinct, their knowledge and their capabilities in general, and we trust that they will take care of us in a like way. Even if it doesn't mean forever, it can still be an amazing experience in the present, and both parties usually leave a relationship as better versions of themselves, having learned and gained something from the experience. In the pinnacle of Ehwaz we see a union so powerful that there is unspoken communication, a knowing of what that person will say next, how they will act, what they need in that moment and being met in all those things.

Communication is key in Ehwaz, whether your relationship is two people in an office, two lovers in a bed, or a horse and a rider together. Although Ehwaz communicates without words, our minds can play tricks on us and second guess meanings. When words have been spoken and communication is clear, it frees the mind of the exhausting guesswork trying to figure out what the other person wants or needs. Clear communication is necessary for a bond that you can be confident in. Having defined roles and purpose allows us to focus on our job and be assured that the other person will fulfill their role also.

In the rune sequence, Ehwaz follows Berkano, the birth of the hero. Our hero has come out of his isolation, his time spent in the womb, the forest where he was protected. He comes now as an innocent, a babe, an animal, back into the world with wide eyes that see everything in a new light. In Ehwaz we learn to love others, ourselves, the world and our mothers unconditionally, as does a small child or animal.

The shape of Ehwaz is two horses with their heads together, noses touching. If you have spent time with horses you may have seen horses using their heads to communicate love. This highlights how Ehwaz's love is of the mind, whereas Gebo was a connection at the hips. The horse is a representation of our animal state, one where we are connected to source energy and our minds are open. Horse energy implies motion and links to Raidho, the chariot. Where Raidho represents the journey, the horse, the connection with another, can be what fuels and holds it together. These two runes are used together harmoniously. I often find people's descriptions of Ehwaz are related to motion and journeys, and could just as easily be descriptions of Raidho, so I leave the aspect of progress to Raidho and the aspect of synergy to Ehwaz

Ehwaz is also seen as a '1' with another '1' reflected back at it. This is thus a representation of the number 11, which is also said to be a number of balance and union. There is also powerful magick in the number 11, as if you see the repeating numbers of 11/11 often in dates, times, phone numbers, etc., these are signs that higher powers are communicating to you and are very lucky. The 11:11 phenomenon is a product of our digital age but shows how magick still works through our modern systems. It is also the number of the Twin Flame union, a New Age concept where it is said two complementary spirits who were destined to find each other come together in a powerful bond that can help heal humanity.

Merkstave, Ehwaz represents disconnect or miscommunication. This is one of the best examples of how to describe a merkstave rune, as disconnection is not the opposite of love. A disconnect is a powerful example of love. When we care so much that we argue, we want our partner to see things from our perspective – we want them to care. This is thus one aspect of love, not the opposite – which would be hate, or not loving at all. It can also show that there is currently an imbalance of power within a relationship, or that you have no one to make your journey with. Merkstave Ehwaz is a good time to reflect on what is important to you and how to create balance. Sometimes it just means now is a good time to spend time loving yourself first. And sometimes, some beings are just better left independent. Ironically, I have found that the most independent humans rely heavily instead on animals for companionship.

20. Mannaz

[man-azz]: the phonetic 'm' sound, as in man, manage, make, more and mind.

Mannaz. Man. Mankind. That which makes us human, that which separates us from the animals. Mannaz is about society, structure, organization and higher consciousness. Mannaz is seen as the divine light expressed in physical form, to drive our evolution closer to divinity and further from the animal realm.

In the progression of the runes we move from Ehwaz, the loving and trusting animal state, and find ourselves now in a position of responsibility. Our hero emerged like a babe from his time of introspection, but he now remembers society, purpose and what it means to be back among the humans. His long journey has given him a depth of wisdom and knowledge that he can now draw from to contribute to the greater society. His bond between horse and rider or between lovers may now become a role to serve others, where the two continue to work together for a bigger picture. This rune is thus a representation of adulthood and all the work that comes with it.

Where Gebo and Ehwaz needed to be differentiated, so too must Mannaz and Wunjo. Gebo was when two people came together and shared gifts, leading to joy and community in Wunjo. Ehwaz, which is now a lasting relationship, leads to Mannaz and greater purpose in society with many people taking on roles and responsibilities to create even greater structures. Wunjo was a small community where everyone is close and has purpose together, but Mannaz is vast and the individual needs can become lost as we work towards an even higher purpose that is not always apparent. Mannaz is not always joyful, but it is purposeful.

To have our cities, our culture, our structures and our higher learning we need many people in many roles. Some people manage food, teach our children, build buildings, heat our homes, create laws, clean sewers, entertain us or develop

technologies. There are almost as many types of jobs as there are people, and though some may take priority over others, all of them are important and necessary for a functioning society. Assigning and co-ordinating this work involves a great deal of organization – sitting in meetings, moving money and scheduling – all tasks related to Mannaz.

Societal roles may sound dry and uninspired, but there is also something greater hiding there. This is what our evolution is; this is what has removed us from an animalistic state in which we had to fight for survival. Not all of it is dry work. Much of it is about higher thought, such as creating great works that can be seen in the future, learning maths and sciences, and reading and writing to communicate across space and time. This is our divinity; this is the power that the gods have imbued upon us to make us something greater.

The shape of Mannaz is that of Wunjo and a reversed Wunjo placed together, highlighting its link to the community rune. But it is also that of Ehwaz with the additional lines from the divine, as in Ansuz. These two lines are said to be rays of light coming from the gods to create man from animal. The divine rays in Ansuz led to communication, words and purpose, but in Mannaz these are now taken and given a lasting, stronger structure that can be relied and built upon. In my painting, I shone the divine light upon a speaker in an assembly built in a coliseum. The coliseum represents structure, the people are humanity and the speaker is our hero imparting his truth in the divine light. Nature is not present here, but our ability to change nature is also part of Mannaz.

There is a Native American philosophy that humanity's purpose on this earth is as caretakers of the plants. This is also a higher role than that of the animals, for though many animals can greatly affect the ecological landscape none do so with the same level of awareness. So Mannaz is also present in indigenous cultures, as farming, building shelters, making clothing and tools, embarking on hunting trips and collecting medicine. These are also highly intellectual skills that bring us past the realm of animals.

There is great wisdom in traditional ways of life also, and one should not assume that advanced modern societies are somehow better because we have advanced technology. Our advanced technological and societal progression have been majorly beneficial but are also what has caused almost every issue in the world today, which is the merkstave version of Mannaz. Too much focus on society and business can cause a great deal of psychological suffering on an individual level. On a greater scale, it causes environmental damage and imbalances of power, such as extreme poverty. An inverse of Mannaz can also mean not contributing to society and running from responsibility.

21. Laguz

[lah-gooz]: the phonetic 'l' sound, as in lake, life, leek, laze and lull.

Laguz. The lake. The leek. Laguz refers to life force energy. Water is the primary source of life on earth, so it is no surprise that the lake and water should be connected in the rune for life force. There is a relaxed, flowing sense to Laguz, as it is another rune of movement, though not of matter but of energy. The leek is a symbol of health also, as it was one of the vegetables grown by the old Germanic peoples and harvesting them in the fall would signify a successful growing year.

The lake, along with any other body of water, is part of the subconscious dream-state language and symbolizes energy. For example, if you dream of a small pond, this is a reference to a small, unmoving source of energy, whereas a massive flowing river is much energy being channelled into motion. That Laguz symbolizes the lake and life energy should thus come as no surprise, as this is again a universal symbol that most cultures would be able to recognize. Water is necessary for all life, from the smallest microbe to the largest whale, and every plant, animal, fungus or bacteria that falls in between. Lakes and wetlands are also species rich and diverse ecosystems full of life.

Laguz is one of the fundamental healing runes, along with Uruz. This works with the leek and health, as leeks and onions are a remedy for cold and flu, and either water or leeks can be used in tandem with this rune to aid in healing. To flow like water is also another layer of importance, as it allows motion and energy to flow through stagnant areas. This can work to free physical ailments, such as blood clots, and is also important for psychological healing.

Water and emotions are also universally linked. Water can take on any state. It can be liquid, clouds, rain, ice, snow, a river, an ocean, a pond, etc., and it can change between those states depending on the environment around it. Emotions should flow

like water and be adaptable to one's environment. But sometimes we get trapped or stuck in one state, and this is when Laguz can help to release those emotions. Tears are a wonderful healing tool for trauma, to move past and let go of held emotions, and it is quite fitting that tears come in the form of leaked water.

The image of Laguz is that of a leek's stalk, upright with a bent leaf. This is also the shape that many lake plants take, such as the cattail. Incidentally, cattails are also edible lake plants used by First Nations, as when you pull the stalk from the ground the roots are similar to the leeks. Cattails also have a healing property as they filter impurities and can be used in ponds to create clear, swimmable waters.

The leek is also a symbol that extends beyond just Nordic origins. The Japanese proverb "a duck with a leek on its back comes" means good fortune. Duck and leek soup is a traditional Japanese dish, and if the duck comes to you freely with a leek upon its back it is offering itself as a free meal. As ducks are creatures of the water this gives an example of the link between the lake and the leek. This Japanese proverb also shows how leeks and luck are related universally. As for the Norse, leeks were the result of lucky growing year.

In Laguz, our hero finally finds his healing. Ehwaz and Mannaz have helped him find a purpose for his journey, and in Laguz he can finally come to reflect on how all the pieces of his journey have come together. In Freya's aett, he had to put in the work to find his tool, crafted himself a life and found joy. But Hagalaz and Heimdall's aett took all that from him and made him spend time in seclusion, to find himself and his light again. Tyr's aett has given him another chance to join humanity and find a new purpose, and Laguz is now allowing him to heal from the wounds he may have suffered in this journey. He can see that everything he lost, and all his steps, have led him to a greater purpose and place. He can now allow himself to flow with confidence.

Merkstave, Laguz symbolizes stagnation. This can be an area that needs healing, mentally or physically. It can also say that you have not taken enough time to relax, and that you need to focus on making time to allow yourself to recharge. Allowing yourself to slow down and go with the flow is important now.

22. Ingwaz

[ing-wahz]: the phonetic 'ng' sound, as in song, rang, thing, bring.[8]

Ingwaz. Inguz. Ing, Yngvi, Frey, Freyr. He is a god known by multiple names, and even as other faces such as Cernunnos in Celtic mythos. He is the fertility god, the divine masculine in the form of grounded earth energy. He brings seed and causes seeds to sprout and burst forth with their magick from dark soils. This is applied not just to physical plants but is a potent magickal rune that allows ideas and plans that have been sitting dormant to now germinate. Use of this rune can help bring ideas into reality and thus has very practical applications in one's work life, as well as being useful for creative people to actualize their visions. This rune can signify that now is a good time to go for that thing you have been wanting and waiting to do.

Freyr is the twin of the beloved goddess Freya and was also very beloved by the Aesir. Both Freyr and Freya are Vanir gods and fertility deities that came to the Aesir as a peace pact between the two worlds of gods. They were both gifted many wondrous magickal artifacts, such as Freyr's ship Skíðblaðnir, that can be folded into a small bag and always finds favourable winds. Where Freya is also a war goddess, masculine Freyr appears more docile, again highlighting the power female warriors had in Germanic cultures with men being more of a strong grounding force. Freyr, in fact, even gives up his flaming sword for his love of the beautiful jotun maiden Gerd. He has a throne in Alfheim, where he is waited upon by the Light Elves. He rides his golden boar Gullinborsti, which was created by the gnomes of Svartalfheim, across the skies, giving sunlight and rain.

Arguably, Freyr has a close connection to more realms of Yggdrasil than any other god or goddess except Odin himself. Freyr roams the upper and middle realms of Asgard, Vanaheim, Jotunheim, Alfheim, Svartalfheim and Midgard, with only the

---

8. Or 'gn,' as in gnosis.

nether realms of Muspelheim, Niflheim and Hel excluded from his wanderings. This makes sense, as fertility was needed for life on the upper six worlds, but the realms of the dead and ice and fire had no need for his life-giving blessings. Indeed, he is slain at Ragnarok by the fire giant Surtr, which might be a myth relating to a natural disaster such as a forest fire or volcanic eruption that destroyed crops.

I once read somewhere that it was Freyr's ejaculate that brought the sown seeds to life, and he was widely worshipped for his blessing upon the crops. Freyr is usually depicted with an erect phallus. Sperm and the seed are synonymous with one another, and Ingwaz is the most important rune for fertility. It can be inscribed on the pots of plants to aide in their growth, carved on a tree in a forest for restoration or drawn on humans or animals for the act of procreation.

Ingwaz is something of a small climax. It is the beginning, but it is also the end. Most seedlings do not survive, as most sperm do not find their mark. It is an act of magick that fertilization happens, or that the tiny seedling ever makes it to becoming a tree. Similarly, most ideas we have, most magickal intentions, never end up coming into maturity. The bursting of the two tiny leaves or a new idea can be a beginning, but it might also the climax if it wilts prematurely. Ingwaz is therefore the rune of potential, but it also marks an ending.

The ending and beginning is where our hero finds himself in Ingwaz. The next rune, Dagaz, will mark the transition, and Othala will be the settling in and returning to home after a long journey. Ingwaz is therefore the climax and the not-quite-end of our hero's journey. Since his rebirth, he has found partnership, a place in society and healing in Laguz. That vitality from Laguz now bursts with potential, as time back with humanity has given him ideas and he sees the life he wants to create for himself and his partner. Ingwaz may represent him impregnating his partner (or if you choose to view the hero as female, she becomes impregnated by her partner), and the next two runes are the transition from bachelor life to settling down and building family.

The seed is the shape of Ingwaz. There are two forms of Ingwaz (◇) and (⟡), the first is just the seed, the second is the seed that has sprouted tiny roots and leaves. I prefer the second because the seed is no longer dormant, it has begun its growth and things are in motion. If you want to focus on dormant potential energies the simpler form will work better for your intention. One should note that Ingwaz might have little roots and branches, but unlike Algiz there is no central trunk, no strength to give this rune backbone. The little seed has only dreams of becoming the mighty oak.

It is good practice to differentiate the Ingwaz sound from the 'n' sound by vibrating 'ng' and 'n' separately. You will find the 'ng' sound vibrates at a higher frequency, like the noise when your ears ring; 'n' on the other hand is a much lower frequency. The high pitched 'ng' sound is said to be from other realms, and you might find your ears ringing when you tune into particular energies.

There is no merkstave version of Ingwaz. This rune is perfect in its shape. There is no downside to potential energy. One could say infertility would be the opposite of fertility, but again I do not see merkstave as meaning a "lack of."

23/24. Dagaz

[day-gahz]: the phonetic 'd' sound, as in day, dawn, dusk, dark, dream or dip.

Dagaz. The dawn or dusk. The tipping point between the balance of day and night, that is in itself neither dark nor light but marks the transition between the two. Dagaz is about shifts that come in wave patterns of ups and downs. This rune tends to mark the end or beginning of noticeably low or high points in life and says that something is shifting. This rune is also the rune of bipolarity and is often in the birth-reading of people who have severe emotional swings and/or extremes of bad and good luck. Dagaz can be used help bring light to dark places, by illuminating the unknown or helping to phase someone out of a depressive state.

The position of Dagaz and Othala can be exchanged. The way I had been taught and use it is that, esoterically, Dagaz comes first, but chronologically Othala is first. So, for most purposes, Dagaz is the twenty-third rune, but when using a calendar or time-based system Othala is. The Anglo-Saxon rune poem places Dagaz as the twenty-fourth rune, but as the Anglo-Saxon runes differ in the number of runes it is not an end-all argument for placing Dagaz last.

There are a few runes that denote time, so let's start by differentiating them. The first was Raidho, which was the path of the sun (as well as physical travel). Raidho is unidirectional forward motion (unless merkstave) and is repeatable. The second was Jera, which is unidirectional, non-repeatable and represents a year and progress through time. Dagaz differs from Jera and Raidho in that it is change that is repeatable and bidirectional; it does not only progress forward but also backward. This is why it is the same shape as a figure eight on its side – the leminscate or ouroboros, that of a serpent biting its own tail.

Tiwaz, the beginning of this aett, was also about balance. In Tiwaz, both the night and day are present in equal parts; the spear is the pillar by which the heavens are held above the earth. Dagaz is neither day nor night, but the point in between and the shift between the two. Instead of the balance of equality in Tyr, we are now going between one extreme and the other. That this is the wrapping up of Tyr's aett is fitting, as the justice and sacrifice made are now fulfilled and the reward will be given in Othala.

For our hero, Dagaz marks the shift into a new cycle. Our story is ending, but it will also begin again due to the cyclical nature of the runes. Where Ingwaz was a climax, Dagaz is the natural de-escalation from that peak. In Othala, our hero will settle into a quiet family life from his wide and explorative journey that he set out on so long ago. He has learned what there is to learn and now has the experience he needs to settle down. He has found his place and partner and is content. Dagaz isn't much of an event in itself, but it marks the transition point where he rides his horse off into the sunset on his journey home.

Dagaz has very strong implications for emotional and mental states and is one of the most useful runes for aiding mental illness. It can help with anxiety, depression, manic states, trauma, PTSD or any other disorder where one finds they feel particularly low. I don't mean to say it will necessarily heal or fix someone's illness, but Dagaz has profound wisdom helping someone ride out the downward waves and can help turn it into an upward one. Dagaz can help one remember that any emotion is only temporary, as is one's position in life. If you find yourself in darkness, Dagaz is the knowledge that the sun *will* shine again someday. This knowledge is something that, when repeated and believed, will lead to empowerment. So, it may not "fix" one's illness, but it will help give them the tools they need to take charge of it.

It is important to remember that Dagaz is the tipping point between two polarities. It is neither day nor night; it is not only dusk or dawn but can be either of the two. We might like to think that it is only the dawn, the bringing of light and a new day and stepping out of the darkness. However, you may sometimes need to pay close attention to what type of shift this is so you can mentally prepare yourself if you find yourself in a dusk situation. It might feel negative to shift into the darkness from a position of light, but Dagaz comes with the promise that the sun will shine again.

My illustration was intentionally made with the purpose of showing the night transitioning into day, the dark moving into a position of light. But the moon is in a position of waning, where it is fading from its brightest to darkest so both transitions are part of this painting. The tides are another important aspect of Dagaz, as these are another natural principle that rides in "waves" of daily and monthly cycles with the moon. The shape of Dagaz is the shape of waves but it is also that of the infinity symbol – the figure eight on its side. This is a universal symbol of balance and the endless back-and-forth between darkness and light.

The other potent magick that lies within Dagaz is the bringing of the light into dark places. This is useful for someone who has been pondering on an idea for some time but can't seem to solve the problem. An unresolved problem is the darkness. But finally, something comes to shine light on the subject and suddenly the problem is solved. This is the "AHA!" moment many scientists experience. Sometimes it can come in mundane places, like the bathroom or a passing conversation, the places one least expects to find it. No matter the source, it marks the shift into the "day" where we can now move forward with our endeavour.

Dagaz has no merkstave position. It represents a neutral point that is neither positive nor negative. It can be scary to shift into a place of darkness but Dagaz is the knowledge that this too shall pass. If we did not have darkness, we would never be able to appreciate the light. Darkness needs to come in balance for us to have our brightest days. Without polarity, everything would just be a boring grey.

24/23. Othala

[oh-thah-lah]: the phonetic 'o' sound, which I believe to be something between the short and long 'o,' but is usually depicted as the long one. This sound is in offer, open, honour, honest and home.

Othala! The rune of the hearth, home and family. In Othala, this is where we honour our roots. Our heritage is important, as we inherit not just genetic information, but physical wealth and spiritual karma that will all shape the being that is us. Othala is the comfortable home where we can kick off our boots and feel safe. This is not just about what we have inherited, but what we are creating for our family to inherit after we are gone.

Othala is the twenty-fourth and final rune (unless you are using it like a calendar, then it is the twenty-third rune). It is the last rune in Tyr's aett, like our reward for the work in these eight runes. This part of the journey has been about our honour, as Tyr is the god of justice. Each ended in a kind of joy; Othala is the joy of family and home.

Our hero's journey is now at its end. We have come far, and learned much, and in Othala we find ourselves now able to rest. Our hero can grow old, have children, tend cattle and love their partner. The sword and the shield have been laid down, hopefully for good, but perhaps just until the next cycle. We will teach our children the ways, but to them they will just be stories and lessons. They too will have to ride out on their own journey some day. So, the cycle is ending, but it is also a beginning. The cozy farm of Othala will breed the cattle of Fehu, and we will find ourselves back where we started so long ago.

There are many philosophical concepts contained in the Othala rune, the first of which is hospitality. Sharing of wealth and your home to friends, family and strangers was a very important virtue to the Germanic peoples. The stories of Odin as

a wanderer among men were plenty, as were the names and faces Odin could appear by. Welcoming in a stranger could well be a test of the god to judge your quality of character. This was also an important virtue for ancient communities, as travellers wandered many days through all kinds of weather on foot or by horse. Death could be certain for those who did not find shelter, and hospitality was undoubtedly a virtue for the sake of taking care of the community at large.

The second is that of heritage. The old Norse word *hamingja* is their word for family karma. It is a large concept that can be summed up by the honour that is passed down through the family. It is inherited through the deeds of your forefathers and relates to your luck and fate. Our family history is often wrought with a combination of good and bad. It is our duty to do our ancestors and children proud by doing the best we can in this life to add positive *hamingja* to the family line. Many New Age practitioners work with family karma through forgiveness and the release of negative energies passed down through a family's lineage. This can allow the individual to move forward in life with less difficulty, and also honours and heals the ancestors who many have caused the damage in the first place.

Last, but not least, is the concept of *innangard* "in-garden" and *utangard* "out-garden." The German word for garden is *Garten* and is used in the word "kindergarten" (child-garden). *Garten*/garden is used as not just a place to grow vegetables, but as a kind of enclosure or space that has been created for the purpose of growing ourselves. Othala represents the *innangard*, the within world, all that which is contained in humanity's dwellings. These are our fields, buildings, crops, roads, etc., and the *utangard* is the outside world beyond that. *Utangard* is the realm of the lesser known which we now just think of as forests, but to the Germanic peoples this was a much broader world that contained trolls, fairies and unknown magick. It was a darker place which was needed and accessed but was known for being dangerous.

The shape of Othala is said to represent a hearth. This is the heart of the home, the warm fire that welcomes strangers and takes care of the family. I also see Othala as an aerial view of *innangard* and *utangard,* where we have the home as the diamond shape and a fenced yard that leads out into the wilderness. This fence is a kind of a funnel to draw people into the home. The bottom portion of Othala is also said to represent roots, like in Ingwaz. This is the relation to our heritage, our genetic legacy and our link to the source energies from whence we came. Othala is very much about roots. I also see Othala as a doorway. This is the separation between *innangard* and *utangard;* it keeps the warmth in and the trolls out.

The cats I painted here were an important piece of a Norse home. Cats were blessed of Freya and were gifted to newlyweds to complete their new home. The cats would take care of the rats and mice that could devastate grain stored for the winter. As anyone who has had to deal with rat infestations in the modern era can imagine, cats had an invaluable role as household protectors and kept some of the dangers of *utangard* at bay. The giant cat breed called Skogkatt was fluffy to survive the outside snows, but was also a worthy adversary for the big rats in Norway. These cats are usually the kind depicted pulling Freya's cart.

Merkstave, Othala represents a disconnect from one's roots. Feeling like you have no home, no place you belong or no family may all be linked to merkstave Othala in a reading. The advice may be to make that connection, maybe even by starting somewhere small and looking into your family history. Grounding is the theme in Othala, and it may be necessary to find something to keep yourself grounded if you find yourself with this rune inverted. It may also signify it is time to pull those roots and find somewhere else to plant them.

Using the Runes

THE ACT OF RUNE READING IS A VERY PERSONAL PRACTICE. Learning the runes takes time and dedication. Reading a book and memorizing the meanings is a good start but that makes you a student, not a practitioner. The imagery and write-ups I have provided should give you a sturdy basis with which to work, but ultimately the work is your job if you want to make the runes a part of your spiritual practice.

This next section of the book will lay out some options for you to create your own practice. It is a summation of methods that have worked for me based on my views. So please, as you read, keep in mind there is really no wrong way of learning and using the runes. It is up to you as to what works best. I may have opinions and methods that don't work with you, and that's fine. I encourage that you do you. The main thing is that you keep at it. Try different things, look from different angles and try to learn what you can inside and out.

Choosing & Crafting Runes

A SET OF ELDER FUTHARK RUNES CONSISTS OF THE TWENTY-FOUR RUNES. These are painted, burned, carved, etched or otherwise inscribed upon a material. The material ranges from branches (either whole or cut into rounds), stone, bone or any other natural material that can be cut into equal pieces. More recently, people have also cast runes in materials such as resin, and runes can be made from a 3D printer if desired.

It's important that your runes be a consistent size and shape, as you don't want it to be obvious which one is which without looking at the marking. For example, in my first rune set the pieces of wood were not all equal and I decided Thurisaz, the giant, would go on one of the larger rounds. Needless to say, I drew Thurisaz more often and I ended up knowing when I grabbed it in the bag.

Something else to keep in mind is the source of your material. Different woods come with different vibrations. For example, a sturdy oak is different from the feminine birch or a fragrant cedar. A living tree is different from a driftwood branch, which will have the energy of water. Runes carved on bone or antlers will embody some aspect of the animal chosen. A cow is different from a deer, and both are quite different than to a bear. Runes made from synthetic materials will lack any of the energies that the natural spirits imbue into them.

How you collect the item is important also, and collection of living materials for runes should be done in ritual with respect to the donor. One method, if you are seeking wood or bone, is to meditate and go on your walk with intent, asking your gods or higher power to guide you to the magickal item you are seeking. This can also be done in trance induced by music or sacrament. Once you have found the material, give thanks to its source and to your guides. Perhaps leave an offering to the spirits for their gift. A good rule of thumb with plant matter is to never take more than thirty percent, and never more than what you will use.

Alternatively, you may have come across your runes-to-be by happenstance while not in ritual. This is fine, and is a form of manifestation magick. You can still honour the animal or plant spirit by spending time with the item before you cut it and carve it, connecting with its source energy and giving thanks. Again, an offering may be given to the forest spirits when you decide to craft your runes.

If you are choosing to craft your runes using modern artistic techniques of casting in resin or printing, you can also do this with intent. Perhaps you are choosing to do so because you do not want to damage plant and/or animal life, and this is a great intention. Just take time to be mindful of why you are doing it, and the magick in your runes will be that of mankind and modern invention rather than connection to earthly spirits.

Gifting is a great way to receive runes. Whichever end of the gifting you are on there is a value and power to the gift itself. I was once told that tarot cards don't have power unless they had been gifted to you, which I don't entirely believe to be true, but I also see the value in it. With runes I think the most power is in crafting them yourself but, for someone starting out and learning, a gift of runes is a powerful way to start. Often, the people who craft and sell runes of crystal or other high-quality materials can provide the most appealing sets, and these are wonderful gifts to give. By purchasing and gifting runes you are also supporting a local craftsperson, which gives back value to the community and is also a form of intentional magick.

Once you have acquired your runes you can further bless and consecrate them. Take them to what you consider to be a holy place, perhaps letting spring water run over them or placing them at the base of an ancient tree. You can leave them to rest in the sun or bury them under a rock and come back for them later. A common and ancient method of consecrating the runes is to blood them with the blood of animal, or yourself. A woman's moon blood may be used for this purpose. You can also call in spirits, gods and other higher powers to bless your runes by whatever ritual you feel best suits this purpose.

A set of runes is an impermanent thing, as they have a life of their own that is limited like any living being. At some point you may feel you have outgrown your runes or are ready to craft better ones. Your old runes can then be passed on to someone else, buried and given back to the earth or burned in a sacred fire. Give thanks for all your runes have taught you and allow their magick to pass on. Plastic here should not be buried, but they can hopefully be recycled into a new item.

This section is primarily on physical sets of runes, but there are two other modern methods of learning runes. The first of these are oracle decks, which have pretty images on cards with symbology that makes rune reading easily intuitive. The second method is with electronic applications, online or through software on phones or computers that generate random runes and show what the meanings of them are. Neither of these methods is as chaotic as a physical set of runes, but they have their own value. See Table 1 for comparison of rune reading methods.

Table 1. Modern methods of rune reading

Method	Description	Benefits	Limitations
Physical Runes	Runes are carved upon physical item such as bone, wood or stone	• Can be handmade • Produce random, chaotic results that give more to a reading • Mystical appearance	• Can lose individual runes • Readings require more skill and learning
Oracle Cards	Cards with images are laid out like tarot cards, but with runes on them	• Most visually appealing • Work well with other oracle card decks • Familiar for those who use tarot • Imagery can help with learning	• Less chaotic in nature • Provide less insight due to structure
Application or Website	A random number generator produces a random rune or set of runes	• Doesn't take up space • Super convenient • Makes learning easy	• Uses algorithm that becomes less random over time • Not truly random or chaotic in nature

Chaos can be seen as either a benefit or a limitation. On one hand, it provides a greater insight outside of the boundaries we want to give the runes, allowing the reader to interpret the universe via the chaos. For example, shuffling a deck of cards is random, but placing three cards in a row is forcing placement on the cards, assigning each a very particular meaning, such as past, present and future. Casting runes onto a cloth has random meanings and motion, the past, present and future positions are often still present but there may be multiple paths revealed, multiple runes at one position, etc. So, reading physical runes also takes more skill to understand what that chaos means and some people might not find this suitable to their needs. However, the more you allow chaos into your reading the more of the web of Wyrd can reveal insights to you; some rune casters do not even think that drawing physical runes from a bag one-by-one offers enough random nature to a reading. While cards and applications with random number generators can be used and provide insight and make learning easier, their use is mostly valuable due to convenience and familiarity. As such, I highly suggest making, or at least buying, a physical set of runes.

Daily Practice/Relationship Building

THIS SECTION WILL BE SHORT, AS IT IS NOT A DIFFICULT CONCEPT OR TASK, BUT THIS IS PROBABLY THE MOST IMPORTANT FUNDAMENTAL PRACTICE TO LEARNING RUNES. They are an alphabet and take time to learn. As with language, if you do not use them often enough you will forget much and find yourself going back to relearn them. But after some time, I think it was six months or so of daily use for myself, you become fluent in their use, enough for reading words spelled out and also their use in divination.

You might be frightened now about how you don't have time to make this a daily practice but worry not, I have an easy one-minute-per-day method you can definitely put into your routine.

The daily practice is simple: you draw one rune per day. I choose to draw my rune in the morning when I get dressed, and during the day I contemplate the meaning of that rune and how it manifests in my day. The evening is also fine, and you can take a moment to reflect on your day and how the rune presented itself. You may have noticed while reading the rune meanings that I sometimes mention how this manifestation happens (e.g. Thurisaz, especially merkstave, often occurring during periods and hangovers), as over time you can notice patterns that emerge. It doesn't mean an entire day is ruled by that one rune. In reality many, if not all, runes will be true throughout your day, but it gives you a point of focus with which to pay attention. Drawing the same rune multiple days in a row gives that rune even more power, so pay particular attention when this happens (though make sure to shake your rune bag thoroughly or dump them and put them back in to make sure you're not just picking the same rune you just dropped back on top the day before). Another good habit to develop is vibrating the noise of that rune out loud, to connect with the raw vibrational energy of it.

With this practice you will develop a personal relationship to each of the runes. It is likely that if you resonate with Thor that you may find Thurisaz is a rune of power for you. For me, I most often draw this rune merkstave, and it is a rune that I find more related to pain and strife. If you find that a particular rune is difficult for you, the remedy is to work with that rune and find the power in it! I've since spent time connecting to and appreciating Thor (though I still think he is a little too silly for me to take seriously) and since we are on better terms Thurisaz comes more often in the upright position, though not always.

An example of a positive relationship with a rune is with Hagalaz. I do well with chaos, so Hagalaz often occurs in tandem with really fortunate and unfortunate events happening simultaneously. I get cautiously excited when I draw that particular rune. But there are also days I have drawn Hagalaz where the literal hail meaning occurs and we have hail that day, so you also have to be open and paying attention to the world, as the runes are not one singular meaning. Another example of building a personal relationship is how I went three months using my daily practice before I drew Laguz, and as this was the last of the runes to show up in my daily draw there was a sense of completion that came with it. It wasn't even until years after that I felt I fully clicked with Laguz, as I was laying floating in a lake and it came to me to vibrate the 'l' sound and suddenly felt the life force flowing.

The relationship building is a slow process, and anyone can learn the runes. Some runes you may click with right away and feel you understand, and some may take more time. They will often trick you though, and just when you think you have mastered a rune another layer of meaning will sneak up on you and the learning process continues. Whether there is anyone who has truly mastered the runes is questionable, but the ones most likely to be called master are definitively the ones who have used them for the most amount of time and have experienced the many different ways each of them expresses itself.

Another act that can be completed daily is to keep your eye out for runes that appear in the physical realm. I've caught them in signs, buildings, twigs, leaves, spider webs and footprints, to name a few. When this happens, the rune is reaching out and asking you to pay attention to it. Most commonly you will just see them and be reminded of their meaning, but sometimes these will come as items that you can take home with you.

There was one Algiz stick that I found and kept in my car as a talisman for safety. After one particularly difficult journey of driving around nine-hundred kilometers on a sprained ankle I had to use for the gas pedal and sleeping in my car because I had no money for a hotel, I arrived safely at my destination but the stick had been broken. One could say the change in altitude or humidity was the physical factor that broke the stick, which is likely the proximate cause, but I see the ultimate cause as the magick of the Algiz stick had been used up on that journey.

Crafting Talismans & Writing in Runes

Once you have some fundamental basis with the runes, the next step is learning when and where to write them. In this section I'll review some of the fundamental uses, namely talismans, using the runes for written script and bindrunes. Bindrunes and talismans are primarily magick in their use, while writing can have the primary focus of being magickal or simply for communication.

Most talismans won't just show up in nature and ask you to carry them in your car. Rather, most talismans are crafted intentionally. Similar to making the runes themselves, these are often carved on wood, bone, antler, stone, etc., or cast using resin or other materials. You can use the same ritual and blessing techniques for the crafted talismans as when you craft runes, with the difference that a talisman has a specific, singular purpose. Is it an amulet for protection? Invoke a power animal for protection or ask the Valkyries for a blessing. Are you looking for love? Imagine yourself in that space when you actually have the love you are seeking and imbue the item with the essence of having that love, not searching for it. There are multiple ways that one can empower a talisman but being specific in your need and the purpose of the item is the best way to get the results you want.

Runes can also be used to empower a ready-made item. Historically, runes were drawn on helmets, shields and swords as blessings in battle. They were also used to mark gravestones and cast spells on trespassers. In the *Poetic Edda,* there is a poem known as *Sigrdrífumál — The Ballad of The Victory-Bringer,* or *The Lay of Sigrdrifa*. It gives a good breakdown of the uses of several runes: to be inscribed on cups, swords, bark and other items. The following is Henry Adams Bellows' translation from 1936:

6. Winning-runes learn, | if thou longest to win,
   And the runes on thy sword-hilt write;
Some on the furrow, | and some on the flat,
   And twice shalt thou call on Tyr.

7. Ale-runes learn, | that with lies the wife
   Of another betray not thy trust;
On the horn thou shalt write, | and the backs of thy hands,
   And Need shalt mark on thy nails.
Thou shalt bless the draught, | and danger escape,
   And cast a leek in the cup;
(For so I know | thou never shalt see
   Thy mead with evil mixed.)

8. Birth-runes learn, | if help thou wilt lend,
   The babe from the mother to bring;
On thy palms shalt write them, | and round thy joints,
   And ask the fates to aid.

9. Wave-runes learn, | if well thou wouldst shelter
   The sail-steeds out on the sea;
On the stem shalt thou write, | and the steering blade,
   And burn them into the oars;
Though high be the breakers, | and black the waves,
   Thou shalt safe the harbor seek.

10. Branch-runes learn, | if a healer wouldst be,
    And cure for wounds wouldst work;
On the bark shalt thou write, | and on trees that be
    With boughs to the eastward bent.

> *11. Speech-runes learn, | that none may seek*
> *To answer harm with hate;*
> *Well he winds | and weaves them all,*
> *And sets them side by side,*
> *At the judgement-place, | when justice there*
> *The folk shall fairly win.*
>
> *12. Thought-runes learn, | if all shall think*
> *Thou art keenest minded of men.*

So, beyond physical items one can see that the runes can be drawn on the body for different purposes. Nauthiz can be scratched onto one's fingernails in times of desperate need. Berkano can be used in birth on the mother's palms and joints. This is by no means an exhaustive list, as the poem lacks some of the pages and is thereby incomplete, but it is a good window into the past of how the runes were used. At the very least, it attests that by drawing the runes on the body one can channel their powers. Tattooing is now a very common form of this, but it should not be lightly or ignorantly done as one would not want to invoke the wrong runes on themselves and tattoos are much more permanent than charcoal or scratches on fingernails.

So far we have just looked at individual runes, but the next stage is writing with them. Words were used in many of the above magickal contexts, such as the ninth-century Sæbø sword, with the inscription translated roughly as "Thor owns me" by George Stephens in 1884. This sword is not only blessed with a swastika that is said to represent Thor, but it also contains a written message. This is but one example where writing in runes was a common historical practice.

Sometimes, the runes were also used just to create basic writing without apparent magickal context, like our alphabet. For example, the inscription on the U 241 runestone, known as Lingsbergsstenen 2, says the following:

> "And Danr and Húskarl and Sveinn had the stone erected in memory of Ulfríkr, their father's father. He had taken two payments in England. May God and God's mother help the souls of the father and son."
>
> (TRANSLATION BY WILLIAMS, 1993)

This stone has a striking similarity to how we mark gravestones, or sometimes create plaques on benches in parks for lost loved ones. There may not be a particular magickal intent in mind, but there is something in the act of writing that still has power to it. Keep this in mind if you choose to use the runes for writing.

There are several ways people today use runes for writing. The first, as we have seen, is in magickal practice. Another is as a coded script, for a small group of people can practice and easily use the runes as a code, of sorts, to send letters that not everyone will understand. The third and most common use by far, I would say, is stylistic. Many people have crafted signatures in runes. Rune script is also used in arts such as tattooing and leatherwork, with writing everything from single words to entire songs, and everything in between. All these uses are valid and encouraged, as the more runes are used, the more people become interested and the more power they will have.

The only real "trick" to writing with the runes is that you should use their phonetic values and not their exact English letter equivalents. For example, the word Thor should be written as (ᚦ ᛟ ᚱ) with Thurisaz as the first rune, rather than the 't' and 'h' as separate letters. One must also keep in mind that Germanic speech has some sound differences from English that don't make transcription easy, so there is a level of ambiguity around certain runes and letters. Some of the more conservative runesters would say that to use rune writing properly, one must only use Scandinavian and German words when writing runes. Others think it is fine to use the runes to correctly spell English words, even though particular sounds do not translate perfectly. Whatever your choice, keep to the phonetics as best as possible, and if you are unsure while learning there are great online groups you can ask for feedback and opinions. Tables 2–4 are an easy reference guide with relevant information for writing, creating bindrunes and determining your birth rune. I created the tarot associations based off my knowledge of both systems and where there is an overlap of meaning; Edred Thorsson has different associations based off of astrology.

Tables 2 – 4. The Elder Futhark runes

Freya's Aett

Futhark Symbol	Rune Name	Phonetic Value	English Letter	Linguistic Notes	Smaller Runes Within[9]	Related Tarot	Calendar[10]
ᚠ	Fehu	'f'	F			• Sephiroth of Malkuth • The suit of Pentacles	June 29 – July 14
ᚢ	Uruz	'oo'	U	Long 'u'	Isa	Combination: • VIII. Strength • II. High Priestess	July 14 – July 29
ᚦ	Thurisaz	'th'	None		Isa, Laguz		July 29 – Aug 13
ᚨ	Ansuz	'ah'	A	Short 'a'	Isa, Laguz, Wunjo?, inverse Kenaz	• IV. Emperor	Aug 13 – Aug 29
ᚱ	Raidho	'r'	R		Isa, Laguz	• V. Heirophant*	Aug 29 – Sept 13
ᚲ	Kenaz	'k'	C or K	Hard 'c'	Isa, Laguz, Kenaz, Wunjo, Ansuz, inverse Sowilo	• VII. The Chariot • 0. The Fool	Sept 13 – Sept 28
ᚷ	Gebo	'g'	G		None – Primary fire rune	• XIV. Temperance*	Sept 28 – Oct 13
ᚹ	Wunjo	'v'	W of V	'w' is like 'v' in Germanic languages	Kenaz	• VI. The Lovers	Oct 13 – Oct 28
					Isa, Laguz	• XXI. The World*	

9. Used for creation of bindrunes
10. Calendar from Nigel Pennick and Freya Aswynn
?. Denotes runes where I am uncertain they fit perfectly due to height or angle but can still be seen within the larger rune.
*. Used where I don't feel the tarot and runic meanings overlap well enough for them to be a perfect correspondence. I.e. The association is weak and debatable.

Heimdall's Aett

Futhark Symbol	Rune Name	Phonetic Value	English Letter	Linguistic Notes	Smaller Runes Within[9]	Related Tarot	Calendar[10]
	Hagalaz	'h'	H		Isa, Uruz, Laguz (Snowflake form contains all 24 runes)	• XVI. The Tower	Oct 28 – Nov 13
	Nauthiz	'n'	N		Isa, Laguz?	• XV. The Devil	Nov 13 – Nov 28
	Isa	'ee'	I	Long 'e'	None – Primary ice rune	• IX. The Hermit	Nov 28 – Dec 13
	Jera	'y'	Y or J	'j' is like 'y' in Germanic languages	Kenaz	• X. Wheel of Fortune	Dec 13 – Dec 28
	Eihwaz	'eye'	None	Not generally used for writing	Isa, Laguz	• XII. The Hanged Man • XIII Death*	Dec 28 – Jan 13
	Perthro	'p'	P		Isa, Laguz	• 0. The Fool*	Jan 13 – Jan 28
	Algiz	'z'	Z		Isa	• XVIII. The Moon*	Jan 28 – Feb 13
	Sowilo	's'	S		Kenaz	• XIX. The Sun	Feb 13 – Feb 27

9. Used for creation of bindrunes
10. Calendar from Nigel Pennick and Freya Aswynn
?. Denotes runes where I am uncertain they fit perfectly due to height or angle but can still be seen within the larger rune.
*. Used where I don't feel the tarot and runic meanings overlap well enough for them to be a perfect correspondence. I.e. The association is weak and debatable.

Tyr's Aett

Futhark Symbol	Rune Name	Phonetic Value	English Letter	Linguistic Notes	Smaller Runes Within[9]	Related Tarot	Calendar[10]
↑	Tiwaz	't'	T		Isa, Laguz	• XI. Justice	Feb 27 – Mar 14
ᛒ	Berkano	'b'	B		Isa, Laguz, Sowilo, Kenaz, Wunjo	• III. The Empress	Mar 14 – Mar 30
ᛖ	Ehwaz	'eh'	E	Short 'e'	Isa, Laguz	• VI. The Lovers	Mar 30 – Apr 14
ᛗ	Mannaz	'm'	M		Isa, Laguz, Ehwaz, Wunjo, Gebo?, Kenaz, Dagaz	• I. The Magician	Apr 14 – Apr 29
ᛚ	Laguz	'l'	L		Isa	• XXI. The Star	Apr 29 – May 14
ᛜ	Ingwaz	'ng' or 'gn'	None	Words ending in –ing, –ong, –ang, etc, or beginning with 'gn'	Sprouted: Gebo, Othala, Sowilo, Kenaz Seed: Kenaz	• XX. Judgement*	May 14 – May 29
ᛞ	Dagaz	'd'	D		Kenaz, Gebo?, Isa?, Laguz?, Ehwaz?	• XVIII. The Moon* • XIV. Temperance*	June 14 – June 29
ᛟ	Othala	'oh'	O	Long 'o'	Ingwaz, Kenaz, Gebo?, Sowilo	• XXI. The World*	May 29 – June 14

9. Used for creation of bindrunes
10. Calendar from Nigel Pennick and Freya Aswynn
?. Denotes runes where I am uncertain they fit perfectly due to height or angle but can still be seen within the larger rune.
*. Used where I don't feel the tarot and runic meanings overlap well enough for them to be a perfect correspondence. I.e. The association is weak and debatable.

Before I explain what bindrunes are, I want to summarize some interesting patterns in how the runes contain other smaller runes. It is important to note that all the runes contain either Isa or Kenaz, the runes of ice and creative fire. These runes are therefore representations of the energies from Niflheim and Muspelheim respectively. These are the worlds of ice and fire from whence everything was created at the beginning of time. The runes are thus all created from one or both of these realms.

Someone once argued to me that Isa is contained within all the runes, including Kenaz. However, I would argue that there are three planes in the web of Wyrd, and Isa is contained within the vertical axis. These axes can be played with for the creation of bindrunes and sigils, so arguably one could see Isa in all the runes. I see of each of the three axes as separate entities when it comes to the structure of the Elder Futhark. So Kenaz, being a combination of the two non-vertical axes, is the second element that makes up the structure of the runes and is separate from Isa.

Laguz is the next most common element in the creation of larger runes, which is life force and water, the flowing and creative form of the ice of Isa. Mannaz contains the most other runes inside of it. This may be because mankind, on our world of Midgard, was created long after the gods and thus contains many of the elements that led up to its creation.

A bindrune is a combination of runes that are intertwined for an intention beyond what a single rune or a written word provides. Usually the purpose is magickal, where you have an intention you want to achieve and you choose runes that will aid in that intention and combine them, such as on an amulet or stave. It can also be a combination of runes in a word, such as the name of a particular group where the runes are then combined to make a single, new symbol.

The best results for bindrunes come from having a singular intention. For example, love and prosperity are two separate intentions and should not be put into the same bindrune. Simplifying this to something like happiness will have a better result, and then you can reflect on which runes will aid in accomplishing this goal.

Going with the example above, let's take a look at what runes you might use and how that would come together. My suggestion would be a combination of Wunjo (literal joy), Sowilo (inner light) and Ehwaz (if partnership is part of your vision of happiness). The result could look something as follows:

Here, the three runes are obvious, and not inverted so as to keep their proper meaning. Ehwaz is a larger rune that can lead to clunky looking bindrunes, but it is more important magickally to keep your meaning and your bindrune simple.

Sometimes it can be more visually appealing to have symmetrical bindrunes, but then you have to be wary of making new, undesired runes. Here is the same bindrune as above, but with a vertical line of symmetry in the center. Now, Othala, and Mannaz have been created within the rune, which changes the meaning and the value of the rune as it now could be a rune about family structure. This could be a legitimate and powerful bindrune, if the intention and purpose were correct, but it would not serve as well for a rune to create happiness unless you want to create happiness through other people.

Worse, you could drop the Sowilo and up with something like this, where now you not only have Othala, but it is inverted, and you have created Raidho.

Another symmetrical version of this rune could be this. However, here we now have created both Tiwaz and Eihwaz. Tiwaz could be a good rune to include in one's pursuit of happiness, but Eihwaz is one that is better avoided unless one wants to spend a lot of time dreaming. So, though this is a visually stimulating rune it also makes the meaning more complex than it needs to be.

It is important to note the runes already embedded within the runes you choose, such as how there is a Dagaz present in Mannaz, Laguz within Wunjo, and Wunjo within Mannaz. Because Mannaz in particular has so many elements, it is important to not include Mannaz unless you are intentionally choosing to, or you end up with a lot of unwanted runes in your bindrune. Taking the time reflect on why and how the smaller runes affect the larger ones is a practice that takes time and should precede any bindrune work. This is why I have included them in Tables 2 – 4. This should help show which runes will inevitably come with the larger ones, so the fact that Laguz appears in the above bindrunes doesn't make it an unwanted rune, but an inevitable one that is linked with Wunjo and Ehwaz.

Hopefully this small exercise impresses upon you that bindrunes are tricky and not to be taken lightly. There are many more fine details that I won't go into about the effects of particular runes in bindrunes, such as how Gebo can harmonize other runes. Each rune has their own little effects like this and needs to be examined very carefully before being combined with other runes. Bindrunes are not a beginner exercise due to these details, as well as the nature of how easy it is to create unwanted runes when combining them.

Rune Casting

Casting the runes involves using them to discern answers to specific problems or questions. The random nature of the runes allows the reader to observe the patterns of the web of Wyrd and answer the question at hand. This is similar to the lessons in Perthro, where the luck and fate of someone could be determined through the fortune they had in game play. Now, the threads of fate are revealed through the runes in a more in-depth type of scrying.

Before I delve into the details of how to do rune casting, I'm going to touch base on how this might work from an objective perspective. The runes are symbols that allow us to tap into our subconscious minds. We can see that as being magick and a way of allowing us to tap into our superconscious. And maybe that is true, but at the very least, using our subconscious brains to answer questions is a powerful psychological tool. This is also magick, and a very important tool in self mastery, as the subconscious mind is not easily accessed by the conscious one. By casting runes and picking out symbols and patterns we advance our practice beyond simple knowledge of the symbols to being able to pick out larger cosmic patterns. This allows us to make more holistic decisions based on not just what our conscious brains are telling us, but also the subconscious mind. Rune casting is thus a powerful tool for tuning into deeper parts of our minds and can be used as a valuable psychoanalytical tool.

When doing rune readings you will likely find the answers the runes give are ones you already knew. These are often difficult lessons that maybe you have been avoiding or do not want to pay attention to. If unaddressed, you will likely find these messages repeat themselves in later readings. The runes are brutally honest, and when consulting them I recommend that you do so prepared to hear some hard truths.

I suggest making an offering and clearing your space using a smoke smudge. Most cultures had some type of smoke/smudge plant that can be used to clear energies from a place (interestingly, most of these plants have antibacterial and healing compounds), and some research and talks with local peoples will help you find a plant you can safely harvest yourself without buying endangered species. Some good traditional European smudge options include cedar, sage (if you pick it or grow it locally), sweet grass, rosemary, thyme, chamomile, angelica or nettle. Mugwort is also a sacred plant of Odin and a great choice for smudging. I like to use sage that I pick from localities nearby. I only take a very small bundle at a time from a healthy plant and give thanks for the gift. I will note here that most sage purchased from stores is white sage, which is currently becoming endangered in its native land, so I stress that you should not buy the general sage bundles from metaphysical shops. Palo santo trees are also endangered and should not be purchased.

The offering for the runes can consist of mead, a kiss, a candle, a prayer, etc. This is about Gebo and reciprocity, being thankful for the answers given and giving something intentionally in return. This needn't be anything large, but intention helps with focus and putting energy into your runes.

One popular method of rune casting involves drawing runes into specific positions, like tarot cards. I touched on this when I mentioned rune oracle cards, as this is the only way that rune oracle cards can be used. For example, you could draw three runes, one each for past/present/ future, or body/mind/soul or situation/challenge/outcome. The rune for each position then gives you insight into that particular part of the reading. Three is an especially good number for rune magick as it also applies to the 3/6/9 principle with nine being the primary magickal number.

For example, let's use an example of body, mind and soul. Three runes are drawn and placed into the three positions while emptying your mind and focusing on yourself, with the intention of tuning into yourself. The runes drawn are merkstave Uruz, Tiwaz and Raidho. Merkstave Uruz suggests being physically unwell, in the body position this is a particularly strong message. The mind position with Tiwaz is a strong place for this rune, as Tiwaz is a rune of air and the mind. It says your mind is sharp and discerning, and to trust your judgement you know what you must do. Raidho in the spirit position suggests movement forward. This is telling you that you are ready for growth and should accept any opportunities to get out of your comfort zone. Overall, the reading suggests that you should pay attention to your physical health (merkstave Uruz) as it may be holding you back from the growth in Raidho. Tiwaz is an affirmation that you know this and need to make decisions in your best interest.

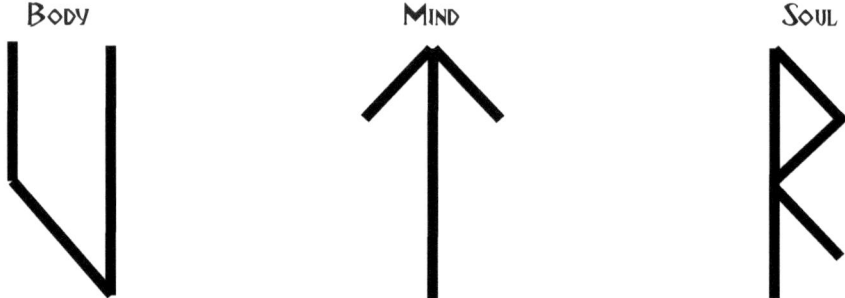

Using runes in these positions isn't my preferred way of doing rune readings, but it is a tried and true method that can be used with very helpful results. It helps to have the defined positions and purposes for getting a clear and legible answer to what you're looking for. I do like the three rune draws if someone receiving a reading wants them. I find that with more than three you start to have too many positions and not enough runes to choose from to give you adequate answers. For example, a Celtic Cross spread with 13 positions or more uses over half of the runes, many of which may not really be relevant in the reading, but you forced the rune into the position. These large spreads are best left for tarot decks with 72 cards, or perhaps if you had two rune sets. I do like some of the ways Freya Aswynn uses spreads, where there are twenty-four positions corresponding to each of the Futhark runes in order, then you place a randomly selected rune on each of those spaces. This gives you insight into each area of your life. For example, health is the Uruz position and if you draw upright Laguz here it suggests good health, but something like merkstave Thurisaz is problematic.

Another way to read runes can be to combine them with oracle decks. I quite like using a spirit animal card deck, as the spirit animal acts as a kind of overall guide in whatever matter is at hand. But any other decks you have can be combined with runes if they work with your purpose. Another suggestion is to do a tarot spread but draw one rune and place it above the spread as an overall energetic reading for the cards in the spread.

My preferred method of rune reading is just a cast with a random handful of runes, which are dropped over a casting cloth. A casting cloth was, by Tacitus's account, a white cloth. I suggest that any neutral colour is also fine, though if you are using something coloured you will want to be aware of what energies that particular colour attracts. A pattern on the cloth is also beneficial, as you will want to know where the center is and how the runes radiate out from that center piece. I have a casting cloth I created in trance that has the lines of the web of Wyrd across it (see figure below), the value of which you will see later. Mandalas are also great, as they have a center with defined sections. Use your imagination and a symbol that calls to you, or even just use a blank cloth if you feel that is best suited to your needs.

The first thing you need for the reading is an intention. What are you asking the runes? What situation is important to you right now? What is it that you are seeking guidance or answers about? Keep this prominent in your mind or ask the person you are doing a reading for to do this. You, or they, then reach into the bag and draws whatever number of runes feels right at the time. They are released over the center of the cloth and allowed to scatter, allowing the random forces of nature to do their work to show the patterns of the web of Wyrd for you.

Some of the runes will likely not be included in the reading – some runes will bounce off the cloth entirely. Others will land face down. Many rune readers will often discard all of the facedown runes, but I have had readings where all runes were facedown, which suggested to me that there was a lot of blockages. Another time, the facedown runes represented one person's perspective and the faceup runes were that of the person asking the question. Use discretion to sort out if facedown runes are included or not. Facedown runes are one example of how people used to tarot might find rune reading confusing, as it is ambiguous on what you might include or not include. Practice and intuition will help you to see the reasons for the facedown runes.

In the next image, I've put an example rune cast. This cast was done about this book, before I launched my crowdfunding, and is featured in my promotional videos for the book, so it may look familiar to some. I'll go through what it means and what my conclusions are based on the reading. The facedown runes have been removed.

The reading is started at the center of the cloth. The center represents your current self or the present. In this reading, Ehwaz is positioned at the center. It is tilted neither upright nor merkstave, which might suggest some merkstave issues are at bay but mostly it is positive. Ehwaz here says that my relationship is a current theme that relates to the question of my book. My partner was very useful in the production of my promotional materials and I am grateful for the time we spent together here as I'm not sure I'd have done as well without him. We had issues come up and it wasn't all smooth roads either, thus the sideways position of Ehwaz was also correct.

Second, you look at directions. When you have two obvious branches it means two choices are ahead and you read each in turn. When you have a straight line like this reading, however, it suggests a past/future link. The center is the present, as mentioned. Here, I equated the top rune with the past and the bottom runes as the future. Again, intuition is needed to sort out the meaning and directionality.

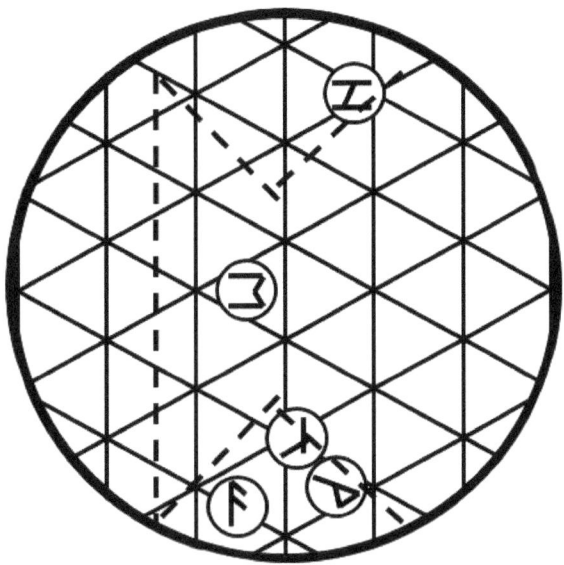

Hagalaz in the past suggests disruption being the causal reasoning for the current situation. This was quite true for my book, as it was borne out of the 2020 COVID pandemic. I would normally have been off at festivals and selling my art but, since I was at home for most of the year, I was given the opportunity to make this book. This is a prime example of Hagalaz at work, where loss and destruction open the way for new possibilities.

The future is a cluster of three runes. We have Nauthiz merkstave, suggesting an unfulfilled need and constriction. Wunjo inverted means a separation from community. Ansuz upright suggests purpose and answers. The result of this suggests that my book campaign was not as successful as I had wanted, and that it would separate me from my community. But it also says that Odin has blessed the endeavour and that there is purpose and a meaning to it. As it stands, it looks like my book will be funded successfully, but not as much as I had hoped to be able to have a higher production of it. I'm also suffering from a need for money beyond that, and the feeling of constriction indicated by Nauthiz is very relevant. At the time I also find myself quite segregated from my community, and there is a distinct lack of festivities. Inverse Wunjo is also thusly correct. So, I would say that this cluster of runes is bang on; I am not currently experiencing much joy but there has been purpose to this process, and I am happy to serve Odin.

One last feature to look at in the reading is the master rune. The master rune is the shape the runes fall into. Here, in dashed lines, you can see the outline of Perthro. Perthro is the rune of luck and fate. Thankfully it is positive, meaning good luck. This rune tells me that this endeavour was one of fate, which is also highlighted by the Hagalaz beginning and the Ansuz end. My book is thus blessed, if a difficult process.

As you can see, the runes did not sugar coat their message to me. Usually a reading will have a mix of positive and negatives mixed in, though I have certainly had some extremely nasty and some extremely joyful readings also. This reading tells me that my book is a significant, lucky and fateful endeavour, but one that will also cause me loss and strife in its creation. That is what this book was born from. Again, if you are a skeptical person you can look at this rune reading as a way to tap into my subconscious brain and things I already know. Or you can look at this as direct communication with external spirits and energies. Either way, the result is the same, and rune reading is undoubtedly a useful and powerful tool when looking for higher insight.

In Conclusion

Isaac Newton is quoted as having said "If I have seen far, it is because I have stood on the shoulders of giants." The same is true for understanding the Elder Futhark, and the knowledge I have to add to the runes. I am, by no means, the first person to create a book on the runes, but with each person that spends time understanding them we uncover a little bit more. The first book I used was Edred Thorsson's *Futhark: A Handbook of Rune Magic* and I will here acknowledge that many of my methods and writings reflect this as my starting point. His writings are biased in their own accord though, and I have defined my own practice. This is probably apparent in my writings.

Runes are a very subjective and personal practice. My book is not the only one out there, nor is it the only one that you should read. Take the time to practice, consult the Eddas, chant the galdr, walk in the woods and honour your gods. If I can give you one piece of advice it is to use your intuition. Your intuition will help guide you away from the people that may have misguided or selfish reasons for teaching the runes and instead direct you to what comes from an honourable place that works for you.

In practicing the runes you will find tools for self mastery. Similar to how some people consult religious texts for their morality and life decisions, by consulting the runes you can receive similar guidance, but without the bias of religious doctrines. They are a spiritual tool that allows you to gain a higher understanding of the forces of nature around and inside of us. Understanding the runes will allow you to better understand yourself.

Spirituality is a part of the human experience. It evolved with us as we separated from the apes. Religions came later as a method of control, a way to capitalize on spirituality. Because religion has been continuously disproved and its damage has been great, the modern world of logic has turned its back on anything spiritual. This has removed us from nature, and instead we use the spiritual part of our brains for worshipping the media and pop culture superstars. But I say we need to go back and find spirituality, to connect with nature and the gods that associate with them so we can become better humans.

Science also has its place, separate from that of belief. Most people tend to go one way or the other, either rejecting science or rejecting any type of belief system. I pose that we allow the two to be separate parts of the human experience. Understand when your mind is working in the spirit realm and don't try to apply that part of your experience to the "real," scientifically discernable world. Maybe one day we will have tools to assess different astral planes and forms of energy, like how measuring sunlight was once impossible. Or maybe the astral planes don't exist in the physical world and are a child of human consciousness. Even if the latter is true, that place is still part of what makes us human and tapping into belief for personal growth makes it a viable psychological tool.

My view is quite nuanced, I often find myself in the middle of two extremist views. This puts me in a place of unpopular opinion by people on both sides. If you don't agree with some of the things I say, that is fine. I think this may be the first rune book written by someone with a background in both art and science. Though it might resonate strongly for some people and bring forth some new and exciting perspectives, I won't be surprised to find myself having long and difficult debates with others after it is published. In some of those debates I will likely also find myself wrong and learning things I did not before, as I am sure that if I wrote this book ten years later I would likely be writing about things I did not know now. This is the way that knowledge grows.

I hope you have enjoyed my artworks and have been able to take away some useful knowledge from this book. This has undoubtedly been the largest project I've tackled on my own accord and I feel quite happy with the results. I greatly appreciate your interest and for supporting me in this journey. May the Aesir and Vanir guide you on yours.

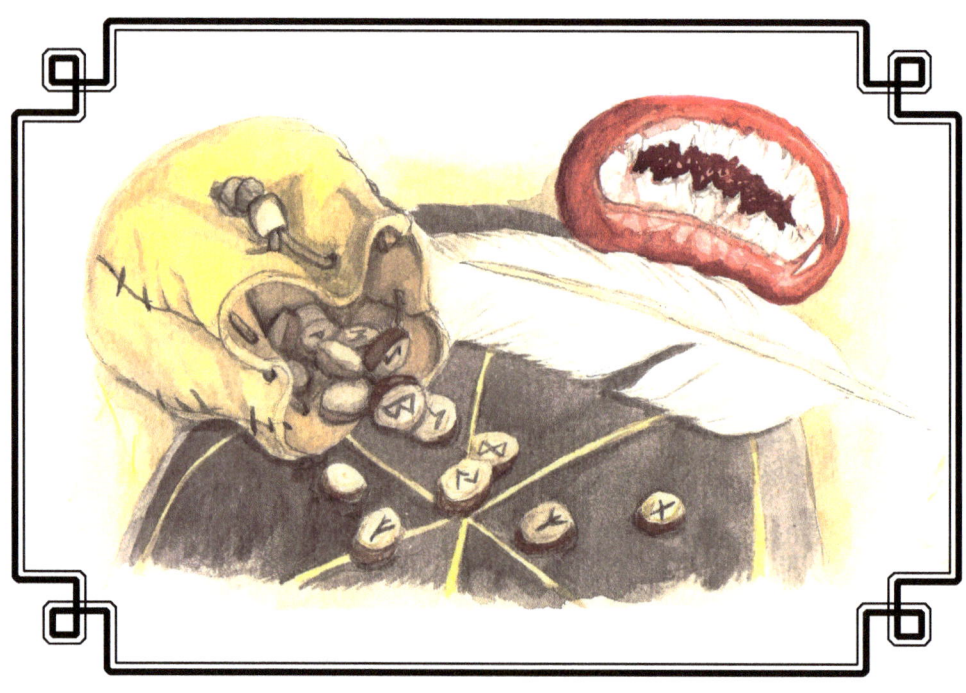

BIBLIOGRAPHY

Aswynn, Freya. (2002). Northern Mysteries and Magick: Runes & Feminine Powers. Llewellyn Publications (2nd ed.).

Bellows, Henry Adam. (1936). The Poetic Edda. Translated from Sveinsson, Brynjolfur, (1643), Codex Regius. Princeton University Press.

Blum, Ralph. (2000). The Book of Runes: 20th Anniversary Edition. London, U. K.: Eddison Sadd.

Brix, Lise. (2015). Isolated people in Sweden only stopped using runes 100 years ago. ScienceNordic. https://sciencenordic.com/language-linguistics-runes/isolated-people-in-sweden-only-stopped-using-runes-100-years-ago/1418110. Accessed September 5, 2020.

Brodeur, Arthur Gilchrist. (1916). The Prose Edda. Scandinavian Classics, 5. Sturlson, Snorri, trans. New York, NY: The American-Scandinavian Foundation.

Byock, Jesse L. (1990). The Saga of the Volsungs. United Kingdom: Penguin Books.

Campbell, Joseph. (2008). The Hero with a Thousand Faces (3rd ed.). Pantheon.

d'Aulaire, Ingri and Edgar Parin. (2005). The D'Aulaires' Book of Norse Myths. NYR Children's Collection.

Dickens, Bruce. (1915). *Runic and heroic poems of the old Teutonic peoples*. The University Press. https://openlibrary.org/books/OL6589060M/Runic_and_heroic_poems_of_the_old_Teutonic_peoples. Accessed Nov 2, 2020.

Gosse, Edmund. (1911). *Runes, Runic Language and Inscriptions*. Encyclopædia Britannica (11th ed.).

Gronitz, Dan. (1999). *The Rune Site*. http://www.therunesite.com/. Accessed Nov 1, 2020.

Harner, Michael. (1980). *The Way of the Shaman*. San Francisco, CA: HarperOne.

Larrington, Carolyne. (1996). *The Poetic Edda*. Translated from Neckel, Gustav, (1983), *Edda: Die Lieder des Codex Regius nebst verwandten Denkmälern*. Oxford University Press.

McCoy, Daniel. (2012). *Norse Mythology for Smart People*. https://norse-mythology.org/. Accessed Nov 1, 2020

McCoy, Daniel. (2016). *The Viking Spirit*. CreateSpace Independent Publishing Platform.

Mountfort, Paul Rhys. (2003). *Nordic Runes: Understanding, Casting & Interpreting the Ancient Viking Oracle*. Rochester, VT: Destiny Books.

Pennick, Nigel. (1995). *Runic Astrology*. Lynnwood, WA: Holmes Pub Group Llc.

Rysdyk. Evelyn C. (2016). *The Norse Shaman*. Rochester, VT: Destiny Books.

Stephens, George. (1884). *Handbook of the Old-Northern Runic Monuments of Scandinavia and England*. Cornell University Library. https://archive.org/details/cu31924026355499/mode/2up?q=sword. Accessed October, 2020.

Stockland, Marie. (2006). *Runes and Their Secrets: Studies in Runology.* Copenhagen, DK: Museum Tusculanum Press.

Tacitus, Cornelius. (1942). *Germany and its Tribes.* New York: Random House, Inc.

Thorsson, Edred. (1984). *Futhark: A Handbook of Rune Magic.* Newburyport, Massachusetts: Weiser Books.

Tyriel. (2011). *Rune Secrets.* Rune Secrets Media. https://runesecrets.com/. Accessed Nov 1, 2020.

Vänehem, Mats. (2010). *Forskning om runor och runstenar.* Stockholms Läns Museum. https://stockholmslansmuseum.se/. Accessed September 5, 2020.

Williams, Henrik. (1993). *Samnordisk runtextdatabas.* Uppsala Universitet. https://www.nordiska.uu.se/forskn/samnord.htm. Accessed October 8, 2020.

www.ingramcontent.com/pod-product-compliance
Lightning Source LLC
Chambersburg PA
CBHW041518220426
43667CB00002B/29